EATCS
Monographs on Theoretical Computer Science

Editors: W. Brauer G. Rozenberg A. Salomaa

Advisory Board: G. Ausiello M. Broy S. Even
J. Hartmanis N. Jones T. Leighton M. Nivat
C. Papadimitriou D. Scott

that almost every ESPACE set has very high Kolmogorov complexity, and then show that every ESPACE hard set has relatively low Kolmogorov complexity. The "simplicity" of ESPACE hard sets is also shown by considering the size of their complexity cores.

The last two chapters are about the Kolmogorov complexity of strings. L. Longpré considers the time- and space-bounded Kolmogorov complexities, and discusses the statistical properties of Kolmogorov-random strings, i.e., strings with the highest Kolmogorov complexity. He investigates the question of whether Martin-Löf's theorem, showing that Kolmogorov-random strings possess all the statistical properties of random strings, can be extended so that it holds in resource-bounded cases. He also relates the notion of Kolmogorov-random sequences to Yao's definition of pseudorandom sequences.

Finally, V. Uspensky surveys resource-unbounded Kolmogorov complexity measures (or *entropies*, as they are often called) that have been introduced in the literature. We should note that one can define several Kolmogorov complexity measures even in the context of resource-unbounded Kolmogorov complexity although their difference vanishes in many cases where the additive $O(\log n)$ factor is ignored. In the pioneering papers of Kolmogorov complexity theory, including Kolmogorov's paper, five basic entropies have been introduced from somewhat different motivations. He explains those entropies from a uniform view point, thereby giving clear understanding their definitions and relations.

References

[Cha69]   G.J. Chaitin. On the length of programs for computing finite binary sequences: statistical considerations. *J. Assoc. Comp. Mach.* 16:145–159, 1969.

[Kol65]   A.N. Kolmogorov. Three approaches to the quantitative definition of information. *Problems in Information Transmission* 1:1–7, 1965.

[LV90]   M. Li and P.M.B. Vitányi. Kolmogorov complexity and its applications. In *Handbook of Theoretical Computer Science*, J. van Leeuwen (ed.), Elsevier, 189–254, 1990.

[LV]   M. Li and P.M.B. Vitányi. *An Introduction to Kolmogorov Complexity and Its Applications*, to appear.

[Sol64]   R.J. Solmonoff. A formal theory of inductive inference, Part 1 and Part 2. *Information and Control* 7:1–2, 22–254, 1964.

Applications of Time-Bounded Kolmogorov Complexity in Complexity Theory*

Eric Allender

Department of Computer Science
Rutgers University
New Brunswick, NJ 08903, USA
allender@cs.rutgers.edu

Abstract. This paper presents one method of using time-bounded Kolmogorov complexity as a measure of the complexity of sets, and outlines a number of applications of this approach to different questions in complexity theory. Connections will be drawn among the following topics: NE predicates, ranking functions, pseudorandom generators, and hierarchy theorems in circuit complexity.

1 Introduction

Complexity theory provides a setting in which one can associate to any recursive set L a function t_L on the natural numbers, and with justification claim that t_L is a measure of the complexity of L; namely L can be accepted by exactly those machines that run in time $\Omega(t_L(n))$. In this paper, we will consider a means of using time-bounded Kolmogorov complexity to define a function K_L, that measures a different aspect of the complexity of L. We will argue that this is a useful measure by presenting a number of applications of this measure to questions in complexity theory.

1.1 Complexity of Strings

Before going any further, it is necessary to define the sort of time-bounded Kolmogorov complexity that we will be considering. Many alternate approaches exist for adding a time-complexity component to Kolmogorov complexity. Sipser [Sip83] and Ko [Ko86] proposed essentially identical definitions, allowing one to define, for each function f, a $f(n)$ time-bounded Kolmogorov complexity measure K^f, where $K^f(x)$ is the length of the shortest description of x from which x can be produced in $f(|x|)$ steps. A related (and much more influential) definition due to Hartmanis [Har83] yields sets of the form $K[g(n), G(n)]$, consisting of all strings x that can be produced from a description of length $g(|x|)$ in time $G(|x|)$. Pointers to other approaches to time-bounded Kolmogorov complexity may be found in [All89a, LV90].

---

* Preparation of this paper was supported in part by the National Science Foundation under Grant CCR-9000045.

The variants of time-bounded Kolmogorov complexity mentioned in the preceding paragraph all suffer from certain drawbacks. For example, the definitions of Ko and Sipser provide a family of measures K^f but offer no guidance in selecting any one function f as the prefered choice when defining *the* time-bounded Kolmogorov complexity of a string x. Additionally, for any given $f(n) \gg n$, the measure K^f assigns the same complexity to a string x, regardless of whether it can be built from a short description in linear time or requires time $f(|x|)$, and thus some important distinctions can not be made. The definition of Hartmanis does allow many fine distinctions to be made, but does not provide a *function* measuring the complexity of a string x; the time and length parameters are not combined in any way.

Thus we turn to another version of time-bounded Kolmogorov complexity: a definition due to Levin [Lev84] (see also [Lev73]).

Definition 1. [Lev84] For any strings x and z, and for any Turing machine M_v, define $\mathrm{Kt}_v(x|z)$ to be

$$\min\{|y| + \log t \ : \ M_v(y, z) = x \text{ in at most } t \text{ steps}\}.$$

$\mathrm{Kt}_v(x)$ is defined to be $\mathrm{Kt}_v(x|\lambda)$, where λ denotes the empty string. Via a standard argument, one can show the existence of a "universal" Turing machine[2] M_u such that, for all v there exists a c such that for all x $\mathrm{Kt}_v(x) \geq \mathrm{Kt}_u(x) + c + \log\log \mathrm{Kt}_v(x)$. Choose some such universal Turing machine, and define $\mathrm{Kt}(x|z)$ to be $\mathrm{Kt}_u(x|z)$, and $\mathrm{Kt}(x) = \mathrm{Kt}_u(x)$.

It is clear that Levin's definition overcomes the objections raised above. However, it may be less clear that Levin's definition is the appropriate definition – or even a reasonable one.

What is the motivation for defining the complexity of x to be the minimum of the sum of the description length and the log of the time required to build x from that description? The answer to this question is that this is precisely the combination of time and description length that is most useful in the study of problems such as the P versus NP question. Consider the problem of finding a satisfying assignment for a formula ϕ with n variables. When searching through all the 2^n possible assignments to the variables of ϕ, what is the optimal search strategy that will lead to a satisfying assignment as quickly as any? The answer, as noted by Levin [Lev73] is to consider each string $z \in \Sigma^n$ in order of increasing $\mathrm{Kt}(z|\phi)$. Levin also used this approach to provide bounds on "speed-up" (in the sense of Blum's speed-up theorem [Blu67]) possible for the problem of inverting a polynomial-time computable permutation.

Levin's Kt function is clearly closely related to the generalized Kolmogorov complexity sets defined by Hartmanis:

---

[2] Levin actually defines Kt-complexity using a different model of computation, allowing the $\log \log$ term to be eliminated; for simplicity, we will stick to the Turing machine model of computation in this paper, as the $\log \log$ terms are insignificant for our purposes.

Proposition 2. $Kt(x) \le s(|x|) \Rightarrow x \in K[s(n), 2^{s(n)}] \Rightarrow Kt(x) \le 2s(|x|)$.

As mentioned above, Hartmanis' formulation has the advantage that one is able to discuss separately the *size* of a string's description and the *time* required to build the string; thus some finer distinctions can be made. However, one of our goals in this section is to define a measure of the complexity of a language, and for this purpose Levin's Kt function combines the time and size components in the most appropriate fashion.

1.2 Complexity of Languages

Now that we have settled on a measure of the time-bounded Kolmogorov complexity of strings, let us consider how to define a complexity measure for languages.

Perhaps the most obvious way to use Kolmogorov complexity to measure the complexity of a language L is to consider the characteristic sequence of L: the sequence $a_1, a_2, \ldots$ where a_i is zero or one, according to whether or not $x_i \in L$, where $x_1, x_2, \ldots$ is an enumeration of Σ^*. Investigations of this sort may be found in [Ko86, Huy85, Huy86, BDG87, MS90, Lut91]. For example, in [BDG87], it was shown that PSPACE/poly is the class of all languages L such that each finite prefix of the characteristic sequence of L has small space-bounded Kolmogorov complexity.

It is often useful, however, to consider the complexity of the individual strings in a language L, as opposed to the characteristic sequence of L. This leads us to the following definitions [All89a].

Definition 3. Let $L \subseteq \{0, 1\}^*$. Then we define:

- $\mathrm{K}_L(n) = \min\{Kt(x) : x \in L^{=n}\}$
- $\mathrm{K}^L(n) = \max\{Kt(x) : x \in L^{=n}\}$

If there are no strings of length n in L, then $\mathrm{K}_L(n)$ and $\mathrm{K}^L(n)$ are both undefined. When we consider the rate of growth of functions of the form $\mathrm{K}_L(n)$, the undefined values are not taken into consideration. Thus, for example, we say $\mathrm{K}_L(n) = O(\log n)$ if there is some constant c such that, for all large n, if $\mathrm{K}_L(n)$ is defined, then $\mathrm{K}_L(n) < c \log n$. Similarly, $\mathrm{K}_L(n) \ne \omega(s(n))$ if there is some constant c such that, for infinitely many n, $\mathrm{K}_L(n)$ is defined and $\mathrm{K}_L(n) \le cs(n)$.

If, for some language L, the function K^L has a slow rate of growth, then this says that *all* of the strings in L have small time-bounded Kolmogorov complexity. In particular, $\mathrm{K}^L(n) = O(\log n)$ if and only if $L \subseteq K[k \log n, n^k]$ for some k. Sets with this property have been studied extensively in recent years; the interested reader will find material concerning these sets, along with pointers to the relevant literature, in the survey article by R. V. Book [Boo92]. Because of this, we will not dwell on the K^L measure, and will focus instead on the K_L measure throughout the rest of this paper.

It is immediate from the definition that for any language L, $\mathrm{K}_L(n) \le n + \log n + O(1)$, and $\mathrm{K}_L(n) = \Omega(\log n)$. The question of how quickly $\mathrm{K}_L(n)$ may grow, when L is a set in P, turns out to have many connections to a variety of questions in complexity theory, and the rest of this paper is devoted to exploring some of those connections, beginning with questions concerning deterministic and nondeterministic exponential time.

2 NE Predicates

Let the complexity classes $\text{DTIME}(2^{O(n)})$ and $\text{NTIME}(2^{O(n)})$ be denoted by E and NE, respectively. These are simply the exponential-time analogs of P and NP, and the E=NE question is generally considered to be of essentially the same level of difficulty as the famous P=NP question.

Of course, much of the motivation for the complexity class NP comes from so-called "search" problems: for example, the problem of searching for a Hamiltonian path in a graph G, or the problem of producing a satisfying assignment for a Boolean formula ϕ if one exists. In contrast to search problems, language recognition problems in NP are questions about the *existence* of solutions. (E.g., $\phi \in \text{SAT}$ iff a satisfying assignment for ϕ *exists*.) In practical applications, it is of little use to know merely that a Hamiltonian path of a given weight *exists* in a graph – it is much more important to have the path itself. The P=NP question itself is usually phrased in terms of language recognition instead of search problems, but it is a well-known fact that P=NP if and only if all of the related search problems are solvable in polynomial time.

An analogous notion of "search problem" may be defined for NE:

Definition 4. An *NE-predicate* is a relation R defined by an exponential-time nondeterministic Turing machine M; $R(x, y)$ is true iff y encodes an accepting computation of M on input x. R is *solvable in time T* if there is a deterministic Turing machine running in time T that, on input x, finds a string y such that $R(x, y)$ holds, if any such y exists.

Stated another way, R is solvable if there is a routine that, for all x, can find a witness for x if a witness exists. Conversely, R is not solvable in time t if each routine running in time t fails to find witnesses for infinitely many x that have witnesses. Note however that non-solvability of R says nothing about the frequency with which "hard" inputs are encountered. Note that the strongest statement about non-solvability of an NE predicate that one could make would be to say that *all* large inputs are "hard" in this sense. This leads to the following definition, which generalizes the classical notion of immunity.

Definition 5. An NE predicate R is *immune* with respect to time $t(n)$ if (1) the set $\{x : \exists y\, R(x, y)\}$ is infinite, and (2) for all f computable in time $t(n)$, the set $\{x : R(x, f(x))\}$ is finite.

The connections between NE predicates and Kolmogorov complexity were first drawn in [AW90]; the following theorem is a slight generalization of the results presented there. In short, it says that there are hard NE predicates if and only if there are sets L in P such that $K_L(n)$ grows quickly.

Theorem 6.

(a) *Every NE predicate is solvable in time $t(2^{O(n)})$ iff for every set L in P, $K_L(n) = O(\log t(n^{O(1)}))$*

(b) *No NE predicate is immune with respect to time $t(2^{O(n)})$ iff for every set L in P, $K_L(n) \neq \omega(\log t(n^{O(1)}))$*

Proof. We will sketch a proof of the first equivalence; the second equivalence is proved in a very similar manner. For the forward direction, assume that NE predicates can be solved in the stated time bound, and let L be a set in P. Let R be the relation given by $R(m, x) \Leftrightarrow x \in L^{=m}$. (Here, we assume the standard binary representation of numbers, and identify a number with its binary representation.) Then R is an NE predicate and there is a function f computable in time $t(2^{cn})$ that solves R, for some constant c. Let s be a description of a machine computing f. Now note that if $L^{=m}$ is nonempty, then $f(m) \in L^{=m}$, and $\mathrm{Kt}(f(m)) \leq |s| + |m| + \log t(2^{c|m|}) = O(1) + \log |f(m)| + \log t(|f(m)|^{O(1)})$, which establishes the forward direction.

For the converse, assume the given bounds on the rate of growth K_L for sets L in P, and let R be any NE predicate defined by a machine M running in time 2^{cn}. Let L be the set of all strings z of length m^c for some m such that there is some prefix w of z such that $R(m, w)$. L is in P, and by assumption $K_L(n) \leq d \log t(n^d)$ for some d. Consider the following routine for solving the NE predicate R: On input m, for each string y of length at most $d \log t(m^d)$, run M_u on input y for $t(m^d)^d$ steps and see if the output produced has a prefix encoding an accepting computation of M on input m. Output the first accepting computation found in this way, if any is found. It is easily verified that this routine solves R within the claimed time bound. $\square$

Corollary 7.

(a) *Every NE predicate is solvable in exponential time iff $K_L(n) = O(\log n)$ for all L in P.*

(b) *No NE predicate is immune with respect to exponential time iff $K_L(n) \neq \omega(\log n)$ for all L in P.*

An essentially identical proof shows that if there is an NE predicate that cannot be solved in time $2^{2^{n-1}}$, then there is a set L in P with $K_L(n) \geq n/5$. We thus see that the most common conjectures concerning the difficulty of sets in NE have as a consequence that there are some sets L in P with rather high Kolmogorov complexity, as measured by the function K_L.

From Theorem 6, we see that the question of whether or not a set L in P can have nontrivial growth rate is very closely related to the E=NE question. It is natural to ask if it is in fact *equivalent* to E=NE. Note that if every NE predicate is solvable in exponential time, then E=NE is a trivial consequence; does the converse hold?

This question was explicitly raised in [AW90] as a result of an investigation using Kolmogorov complexity as a tool for answering certain questions concerning classes of sets equivalent to tally sets[3] under varying notions of reducibility. (See [Boo92] for a discussion.) The question was essentially answered by Impagliazzo and Tardos [IT89]; they present an oracle relative to which E=NE but there are NE predicates that cannot be solved in exponential time. Thus the equivalence of the language recognition and witness-finding problems as it relates to the P versus NP problem does not generalize to larger time bounds.

3 Related Notions

The questions of whether or not $K_L(n) = O(\log n)$ or $K_L(n) \neq \omega(\log n)$ for all L in P have been asked many times by different researchers studying apparently unrelated topics. In this section, we will gather some of these diverse results together.

3.1 P-Printability

A set L is *P-printable* if there is an algorithm that can list all of the elements of $L^{=n}$ in time polynomial in n. An immediate consequence of this definition is that all P-printable sets are sparse and are in P. However, it is suspected that there are sparse sets in P that are not P-printable. P-printable sets were defined in [HY84] and have been studied in many papers; for further information see [Boo92]. It was shown in [AR88] (see also [HH88]) that L is P-printable iff L is in P and $K^L(n) = O(\log n)$.

Many of the papers that consider P-printable sets ask if every infinite set in P has an infinite P-printable subset. It is an easy observation that a set L in P has an infinite P-printable subset iff $K_L(n) \neq \omega(\log n)$. Furthermore, it was observed by Russo (see [AR88]) that sets in NP are similar to sets in P in this regard: every set in P has an infinite P-printable subset iff every set in NP has an infinite P-printable subset. Rephrasing Russo's observation in terms of Kolmogorov complexity, we get:

Theorem 8.

(a) $K_L(n) \neq \omega(\log n)$ for all L in P iff $K_L(n) \neq \omega(\log n)$ for all L in NP
(b) $K_L(n) = O(\log n)$ for all L in P iff $K_L(n) = O(\log n)$ for all L in NP

3.2 Ranking

The property of having an infinite P-printable subset was called "tangibility" in [HR90]. It was studied there as a very weak notion related to a concept known as *ranking*. As there are other connections with ranking to explore, let us consider ranking more closely.

---

[3] A set is a *tally* set if it is a subset of 0^*.

Definition 9. Let L be a language. The function defined by $rank_L(x) = \|\{y \in L : y \le x\}\|$ is known as the *ranking function* for L. (Here, $\le$ denotes lexicographic order.)

If L has an easily-computed ranking function, then there is an efficiently-computable bijection from L onto the natural numbers; each element of L is mapped to its rank in L. This bijection may be thought of as mapping each element of L to a "compressed" representation. If L contains only a small fraction of the words of each length and has an easily-computed ranking function this clearly places bounds on the Kt-complexity of any string in L. Ranking functions were first studied in [GS91] in connection with data compression. Other material on ranking may be found in [All85, BGS91, BGM90, Huy90a, HR90]. A number of classes of sets (including the unambiguous context-free languages [GS91]) have been shown to have easy ranking functions.

If L has an easy ranking function, then a simple binary search procedure enables one to quickly locate the lexicographically least element of $L^{=n}$. It thus follows that any such L has $K_L(n) = O(\log n)$. Thus all the classes of sets shown in [All85, BGS91, BGM90, Huy90a, GS91] to have easy ranking functions are also classes of sets with low K_L complexity.

It is worth noting, however, that the class of sets in P with low K_L complexity is somewhat larger than the class of sets with easy ranking functions. For example, it is not hard to see that if L is a context-free language, then $K_L(n) = O(\log n)$. (The proof is quite similar to the proof of Theorem 4 in [AR88]; see also [All85, Huy90b].) However, it was shown in [Huy90a] that if $P \ne PP$ there are context-free languages that have hard ranking functions. As another example, it was shown in [Huy90a] that if every set in NTIME($\log n$) has an easy ranking function,[4] then $P = PP$, although Gore has observed [Gor90] that $K_L(n) = O(\log n)$ for all $L \in$ NTIME($\log n$). On the other hand, Huynh's techniques [Huy90a] can easily be used to prove that there are sets $S \in$ coNTIME($\log n$) with $K_S \ne O(\log n)$ unless $K_L(n) = O(\log n)$ for all $L \in$ P (which is to say, unless all NE predicates are solvable in exponential time).

3.3 Invertibility

Note that finding an element of $L^{=n}$ is roughly the same as computing a sort of inverse of the characteristic function of L, χ_L; the aim is to find a string in a certain range that is in $\chi_L^{-1}(1)$. In [All85] a number of classes of automata are exhibited that compute only easy-to-invert functions.[5] If L is a language accepted by any machine in one of these classes, then $K_L(n) = O(\log n)$.

---

[4] In order to consider sublinear running times, the Turing machine model considered here has an "index tape" allowing the machine to access a given input position in unit time. This model is commonly used when using the Turing machine formalism to characterize circuit complexity classes.

[5] In a related result, some of these same classes of machines were shown in [KGY89] to be unable to compute pseudorandom generators.

The connection to invertible functions was stated more precisely in [AW90]. It is shown there that $K_L(n) = O(\log n)$ for all $L \in P$ iff every honest function $f : \Sigma^* \to 0^*$ computable in polynomial time is weakly invertible.[6]

3.4 Generation

In work originally motivated by the problem of generating test data for heuristic testing and evaluation, Sanchis and Fulk [SF90] defined the notion of a *polynomial-time constructor (PTC)* for a language L, which is a routine running in polynomial time that on input 1^n either produces an element of $L^{=n}$ or announces that $L^{=n} = \emptyset$. Clearly, if L has a PTC, then $K_L(n) = O(\log n)$, and if L is in P, then L has a PTC iff $K_L(n) = O(\log n)$. (Additional work dealing with constructors is reported in [Huy90b].)

It is noted in [SF90] that most "natural" sets of interest in practical situations are easily seen to have PTCs. Thus sets L in P such that K_L grows rapidly seem to be somewhat "unnatural" – but note that such sets must exist, unless E=NE.

4 Pseudorandom Generators

A pseudorandom generator is an efficient algorithm that takes a short input (the *random seed*) and produces a long pseudorandom output. A pseudorandom generator is *secure* if the output produced passes all "feasible" statistical tests for randomness. Pseudorandom generators are the object of much study in the theory of cryptography; an excellent introduction to the theory of pseudorandom generators may be found in [BH88].

There are many different ways of formalizing the hypothesis "secure pseudorandom generators exist", depending on the particular notion of statistical test being used, and depending on the desired degree of "security". In this overview, we will try to present material on an intuitive level; the reader is invited to consult the cited references for more precise definitions.

For the purposes of this section we will use the definitions of [Yao82]. A statistical test is a language L in P/poly (that is, a set accepted by a (possibly nonuniform) family of polynomial-size circuits). For each input length n, the probability that L contains a random input of length n is simply $\|L^{=n}\|/2^n$. If a pseudorandom generator f takes inputs of length n and produces output of length $p(n)$, then the probability that L contains a pseudorandom input of length $p(n)$ is $\|\{y \in \Sigma^{=n} : f(y) \in L\}\|/2^n$. The generator f will be said to pass the statistical test L if for all polynomials q and for all large n, the probabilities that L contains random and pseudorandom strings of length $p(n)$ differ by at most $1/q(n)$. If f passes all statistical tests in P/poly, then f is said to be *secure*. That is, f is secure if the pseudorandom output it produces "looks random" to all tests in P/poly.

---

[6] A function f is *honest* if $|f(x)|$ is polynomially related to $|x|$; f is *weakly invertible* if there is a function g computable in polynomial time such that $f(g(x)) = x$ for all x in the image of f.

In [All89a], it was shown that most ways of formalizing the hypothesis that secure pseudorandom generators exist have as a consequence that $K_L(n)$ grows slowly for all dense sets L in P.[7] For the purposes of this section, the following result is illustrative.

Theorem 10. [All89a] *If there are pseudorandom generators that are secure against P/poly statistical tests, then $K_L(n) = O(n^\epsilon)$ for all dense sets L in P/poly, and for all $\epsilon > 0$.*

Variants of Theorem 10 were used in [All89a] to show new inclusion relations among complexity classes, under various assumptions about the security of pseudorandom generators.

It is known that pseudorandom generators exist if and only if one-way functions exist that are hard to invert over a significant fraction of their range [ILL89, Hås90]. Thus the existence of this sort of one-way function implies that K_L *cannot* grow too quickly for any dense set L in P. On the other hand, we saw in the preceding section that the solvability of NE predicates was also equivalent to the existence of a certain sort of one-way function, and the existence of this sort of one-way function implies that K_L *must* grow quickly for some sets L in P. Thus there seems to be some sort of trade-off concerning what notions of one-way-ness are mutually compatible; this situation is still only poorly understood.

Taken together, Theorems 6 and 10 motivate the question of whether or not there is any connection between the density of a set L in P and the rate of growth of $K_L(n)$. That is,

- NE contains hard sets $\Rightarrow$ $K_L(n)$ grows quickly for some set L in P.
- Secure pseudorandom generators exist $\Rightarrow$ $K_L(n)$ grows slowly for all dense sets L in P.

Since the left hand sides of these implications are often conjectured to hold, it follows that it is conjectured that $K_L(n)$ can achieve a faster growth rate if L is sparse than if L is dense.

Apart from observations such as these, there is little to guide one's intuition in questions concerning the K_L complexity of sets L in P. In the following paragraphs, we turn to the study of random and generic oracles for help in hypothesis formation.[8]

4.1 Random and Generic Oracles

The study of random oracles in complexity theory was initiated in [BG81]. There, among other results, it was shown that with probability one, $P^A \neq NP^A$, relative

---

[7] In the following, the *density* of a set L, denoted $d_L(n)$, is the function given by $d_L(n) = \|\{L^{=n}\}\|/2^n$. A set L is said to be *dense* if for some k and all large n, if $L^{=n} \neq \emptyset$, then $d_L(n) \geq 1/n^k$. That is, L is dense if it contains many strings of length n, if it contains any at all.

[8] Some of the material in Section 4.1 originally appeared in [All89b].

to a random oracle A. More formally, if we consider a probability space of all oracles over the alphabet $\Sigma = \{0,1\}$, where for each string x the event $x \in A$ has probability one half and these probabilities are independent of each other, then the set of all oracles A relative to which P $\neq$ NP has measure one. Bennett and Gill observed in [BG81] that for most complexity-theoretic statements C of interest (e.g., for C equal to any of the statements "P=BPP," "P=NP $\cap$ coNP," etc.), the set of oracles relative to which C holds satisfies Kolmogorov's zero-one law (see, e.g., [Oxt80](Theorem 21.3)). As a consequence, for statements C of this sort, either C holds with probability one or with probability zero, relative to a random oracle.

Bennett and Gill went on to conjecture that complexity theoretic statements that hold with probability one relative to a random oracle also hold in the unrelativized case. Although their conjecture has been disproved [Kur83, HCRR90, CGH90], it is at least true that the study of complexity-theoretic statements that hold relative to a random oracle provides an internally consistent world view, which sometimes seems useful in gaining intuition concerning the unrelativized case.[9] Thus we will examine the K_L complexity of sets L in P, relative to random oracles.

An alternative to random oracles is provided by the notion of "generic" oracles. Generic sets arise in set theory, logic, and computability, as examples of sets that simultaneously satisfy all properties that can be guaranteed via certain types of diagonalization arguments. They also arise from the use of Baire category to describe a topological notion of "typical set," analogous to the measure-theoretic notion of randomness. The following paragraphs provide a brief introduction to genericity; the reader is encouraged to consult the cited references for more detailed discussions.

The fundamental notion of Baire category is the concept of a *nowhere-dense* set; a set C (on the real line, say) is nowhere-dense if it is "full of holes" in the sense that for every interval I there is a subinterval J contained in the complement of C. (The classic example of a nowhere-dense set is the Cantor "excluded middle" set; nowhere dense sets should intuitively be thought of as being "small" in some sense.) For our purposes, the nowhere-dense sets C we will be considering will be sets of oracles, and intervals correspond to sets of oracles, all of which agree on some finite initial segment. Thus C is nowhere-dense if for every finite oracle F, there is a finite extension $F' \supseteq F$ such that every extension of F' is in the complement of C. This corresponds to the classical definition (e.g., as presented in [Oxt80]), but for our purposes we will want to require that the function (called an *extension function*) that produces F' from input F be describable in first-order logic, or even be computable. A development along this line leads to notions of effective and resource-bounded category (see [Meh73, Lut90, Fen91]). Let Δ be a class of extension functions. Then an oracle G is Δ-*generic* if G is not an element of any Δ-nowhere-dense set. Equivalently,

---

[9] A number of other papers discuss in depth the interpretation that should be given to results concerning random oracles. The reader is referred to [KMR89, KMR91, Cai89, Boo91].

G is Δ-generic if for all extension functions $h \in \Delta$, there is some finite oracle F such that $h(F)$ is an initial segment of G.

Many diagonalization arguments can be modelled in terms of extension functions. For example, a typical diagonalization argument proceeds in stages, with $F_0 = \emptyset$ at stage 0, and then, given any finite oracle F_i at the start of stage i, the argument shows how to build an extension F_{i+1} satisfying some property. That is, the construction is the description of an extension function. Furthermore, if Δ is a class of extension functions (such as the class of extension functions describable in first-order logic, the class of recursive extension functions, etc.) and if G is Δ-generic, then G satisfies all properties that can be ensured via diagonalization arguments in Δ. For example, if Δ is the class of recursive extension functions and G is Δ-generic, then $\mathrm{P}^G \neq \mathrm{NP}^G \neq \mathrm{coNP}^G$ (because the standard diagonalization argument showing the existence of oracles satisfying this property [BGS75] can be modelled in this way). Different notions of genericity (for different classes Δ) have been studied by [Maa82, AFH87, Dow82, Poi86, BI87, Fen91]. Observe that if $\Delta \subseteq \Delta'$, then G Δ'-generic implies G Δ-generic.

In [BI87] Blum and Impagliazzo promoted the study of complexity classes relative to generic oracles specifically as an alternative to random oracles. (They focused primarily on the notion of genericity that results when Δ is the class of extension functions expressible in the first-order theory of arithmetic; for the rest of this paper, "generic" will mean Δ-generic for this choice of Δ.)

As with random oracles, generic oracles offer a consistent world view, in that all "reasonable" complexity theoretic statements $\mathcal{C}$ either hold relative to all generic oracles or hold relative to no generic oracle. In [BI87], Blum and Impagliazzo make the case that generic oracles are perhaps more likely than random oracles to give correct intuition concerning inclusions among complexity classes; they prove a number of theorems to support this case. They also show that it will be impossible to determine if certain questions (such as $\mathrm{P} = \mathrm{NP} \cap \mathrm{coNP}$) hold relative to a generic oracle, without first solving some related questions in the *unrelativized* case. In fact, at the time of this writing, there is no statement $\mathcal{C}$ concerning inclusions among "familiar" complexity classes that is known to hold relative to a generic oracle and known not to hold relative to a random oracle, or vice-versa. Furthermore, the statements $\mathcal{C}$ that are shown in [HCRR90, CGH90] to hold relative to a random oracle but to be false in the unrelativized case, also hold relative to generic oracles. That is, neither random nor generic oracles give reliable information about which statements hold in the unrelativized case.

The reader is certainly asking "Then why consider random and generic oracles at all?"

Our purpose here is to investigate the question of whether or not there is any relationship between the density of a set L in P and the upper bounds that one can prove on K_L. We have seen above that certain popular conjectures indicate that such a relationship does exist. We shall see below that relative to a random oracle there is in fact a *very* close relationship between the density of a set L in P and the growth rate of K_L. On the other hand, relative to a generic oracle there is *no* such relationship at all. We leave the interpretation of these results

to the reader; let us just mention here, however, that we conjecture that one of
these extremes actually holds in the unrelativized case. That is, we believe that
either there is a *close* connection between density and Kolmogorov complexity
of sets, or there is *no* connection at all.

Theorem 11. *For a large class of functions f, relative to a random oracle A:*

(a) $(L \in P^A/poly \text{ and } d_L(n) \geq 1/f(n)) \Rightarrow K_L^A(n) \leq \log f(n) + O(\log n).$
(b) $\exists L \in P^A, \ d_L(n) \geq 1/f(n) \text{ and } K_L^A(n) \geq (\log f(n))/5 \ - \ 2\log n.$

(That is, relative to a random oracle, sets L of density $1/f(n)$ can have $K_L(n)$ no
greater than about $\log f(n)$, and the bound is relatively tight. In the statement
of this theorem, K_L^A is simply the function that one obtains from the definition
of K_L, where the universal machine has access to the oracle A.)

Proof. In order to prove part 1, it suffices to show that, for all $\delta > 0$, the set of
oracles $\mathcal{C}$ has measure less than δ, where

$$\mathcal{C} = \{A \ : \ \exists L \in P^A/poly \ \ d_L(n) \geq 1/f(n) \text{ and } \\ \forall c \exists^\infty n \ K_L^A(n) > \log f(n) + c\log n\}.$$

The idea of the proof is to show that if a machine accepts very many strings
relative to a random oracle, then we can find some accepted string "encoded" in
the oracle, in the following sense. Given the numbers n and r, one can query an
oracle about membership for the strings

$$y_{2^n+rn+1}, y_{2^n+rn+2}, \ldots, y_{2^n+rn+n},$$

where $y_1, y_2, \ldots$ is a lexicographic enumeration of Σ^*. These n queries return n
answers from the oracle, and these answers can be concatenated to form a string
w that can be said to be "encoded" in the oracle, with index $\langle n, r \rangle$. Thus w has
relatively low Kt-complexity, relative to the oracle. (The actual encoding used
will vary only slightly from this.)

Let δ be given, and let $D = \log(1/\delta)$. In the following discussion, assume
that $M_1, M_2, \ldots$ is an enumeration of polynomial-time oracle Turing machines,
where M_i runs in time $n^i + i$.

Define $E_{i,n} = \{A :$ there is an "advice" string z of length n^i with which
M_i^A accepts $\geq 2^n/f(n)$ strings of length n and does not accept any of the
$f(n)(i + n + D)$ strings of length n given by the characteristic sequence of A
starting at $0^{n^i+i+1}\}$. That is, $A \in E_{i,n}$ if the oracle machine M_i, given some
advice string z for the strings of length n, accepts many strings of length n,
but nonetheless manages to avoid accepting any of the strings that are stored in
the "table" encoded by the oracle at position 0^{n^i+i+1}. Since the strings encoded
in this "table" can't actually be read by M_i on inputs of length n (because it
doesn't have time to query the oracle about strings of that size), acceptance
of each one of those strings occurs with probability at least $1/f(n)$ (since M_i
is accepting at least a fraction of $1/f(n)$ of the strings of length n). It follows

that each $E_{i,n}$ has measure at most $(1 - \frac{1}{f(n)})^{f(n)(i+n+D)} < 2^{-(i+n+D)}$. Thus $\bigcup_{i,n} E_{i,n}$ has measure less than $< \delta$.

Note that each of the $f(n)(i + n + \log \delta)$ strings of length n encoded in A starting at 0^{n^i+i+1} can be described relative to A by the pair $\langle n, j \rangle$ for some $j \leq f(n)(i + n + \log \delta)$, and thus any such string has Kt^A complexity bounded by $O(\log n) + \log f(n) + O(1)$. Thus $A \in \mathcal{C}$ implies there is some i such that for infinitely many n there is an "advice" string z of length n^i on which M_i^A accepts at least $2^n/f(n)$ strings of length n but does not accept any of the strings appearing soon after 0^{n^i+i+1} in the encoding given by A. Thus $\mathcal{C} \subseteq \bigcup_{i,n} E_{i,n}$. The result follows.

To see part 2, note that, with probability one, there is a set B in $\mathrm{NTIME}^A(2^n)$ that has no infinite subset in $\mathrm{DTIME}^A(2^{2^{n-1}})$ [BG81, Gas87]. It follows that the corresponding NE predicate is immune with respect to $\mathrm{DTIME}^A(2^{2^{n-1}})$, and thus, as we observed earlier, with probability one there is a set C in P^A with $\mathrm{K}_C^A(n) \geq n/5$ for all large n such that $\mathrm{K}_C^A(n)$ is defined.

Now let f be any easy-to-compute function of the form $f(n) = 2^{g(n)}$, and let $L = \{y : y = xz$ for some $z \in C$ with $|z| = g(|y|)\}$ Then $d_L(n) \geq 1/f(n)$, and $K_L(n) \geq g(n)/5 - 2 \log n$. $\qquad\qquad\square$

In [All89a], some hope is held out that it might be possible to show that there are relatively dense sets L in P/poly such that $\mathrm{K}_L(n)$ grows somewhat quickly. (There would have been interesting consequences for the theory of pseudorandom generators, if such sets could have been shown to exist.) The preceding theorem dashes these hopes (at least as far as relativizing proof techniques are concerned), since the sort of bounds that [All89a] discussed the possibility of exceeding are exactly the bounds shown above to hold relative to a random oracle.

Theorem 11 shows that, relative to a random oracle, there is a very close relationship between the density of a set and the achievable Kt-complexity of the simplest elements of the set. Next we shall see that, relative to a generic oracle, no such relationship exists.

Theorem 12. *Relative to a generic oracle A,*

(a) *There is set L in P^A such that, for infinitely many n, $d_L(n) \geq 1 - 2^{-n/2}$ and $K_L^A(n) \geq n/4$.*

(b) *For all infinite L in P^A, $K_L^A(n) \neq \omega(\log n)$.*

Thus, relative to a generic oracle, there are sets L that, for infinitely many n, contain many strings of length n, but only contain complex strings of length n. However, every infinite set in P^A contains infinitely many simple strings.

Proof. Part 2 follows from a proof very similar to that of Theorem 2.7 in [BI87].

To see part 1, we let L be the generic oracle A itself. Thus, we need to show that, for a generic oracle A, there are infinitely many n such that $d_A(n) \geq 1 - 2^{-n/2}$, and $\mathrm{K}_A^A(n) \geq n/4$.

Let G be any finite oracle. Let n be chosen so that G has no string of length n or greater. For all strings w of length $\leq n/4$, run $M_u^G(w)$ for $2^{n/4}$ steps, and let Q

be the set of strings output or queried by M_u during any of these computations. Note that $\|Q\| \leq 2^{n/2}$ Let $G' = G \cup \{x \in \Sigma^n : x$ is not in $Q\}$. By construction, G' contains many strings of length n, but contains no string of length n with Kt^A-complexity $\leq n/4$. It follows by the results and definitions of [BI87] that, since any finite oracle can be extended in this way, any generic oracle has the properties claimed in the statement of the theorem. $\qquad\square$

Corollary 13. *Relative to a generic oracle, there is no pseudorandom generator that is secure against P/poly adversaries.*

Proof. It follows easily from the preceding theorem that relative to a generic oracle A there is a dense set L in $\mathrm{P}^A/\mathrm{poly}$ such that $\mathrm{K}_L^A(n) \geq n/4$ for infinitely many n. The result now follows from Theorem 10. $\qquad\square$

Although we turned to generic and random oracles in order to find help in guiding our intuition concerning the likely behavior of the functions K_L for sets L in P and P/poly, the results of this section have given contrary indications. It is still far from clear how one might expect the K_L complexity of sets L in P to behave.

5 Circuit Complexity

Recently, Kolmogorov complexity has been used as a tool in proving some new results in the area of circuit complexity; we will review these developments in this section. First let us present some basic definitions. (For more background on circuit complexity the reader is referred to the excellent exposition in [BS90].)

A language L is said to be accepted by a family of circuits $\{C_n\}$ if each circuit C_n takes inputs of length n, and for each x of length n, $x \in L$ iff C_n outputs 1 when given input x. The size of a circuit is the number of gates, and the depth of a circuit is the length of the longest path from input to output.

The class AC^0 is the class of languages that can be recognized by families of circuits of polynomial size and constant depth, where these circuits consist of unbounded fan-in AND and OR gates. Powerful combinatorial lower bound techniques have been developed in [Hås86] (among others), showing that many very simple sets (notably the set PARITY consisting of all strings with an odd number of 1s) cannot be computed by constant depth circuits of such gates of less than exponential size.

Although AC^0 is a very "weak" complexity class in some sense, note that using the definition given above, AC^0 contains nonrecursive sets. (For example, there are nonrecursive tally sets, and every tally set is trivially in AC^0.) These pathological examples can be avoided by restricting our attention to "uniform" circuit families: i.e., families $\{C_n\}$ such that the function $n \mapsto C_n$ is "easily computable" in some sense. The issue of choosing the correct notion of uniformity for AC^0 has been addressed by [BIS90]. Throughout the rest of this paper, we will consider only "uniform" AC^0.

In light of the impressive lower bound results that have been proved, showing that various languages are not in AC^0, it is natural to wonder if stronger separations of P and AC^0 can be proved. For instance, is there a set in P that has no infinite subset in AC^0? (Such a set is said to be *immune* to AC^0.) In most cases in complexity theory, if a complexity class $\mathcal{C}_1$ can be shown to properly contain a complexity class $\mathcal{C}_2$, then $\mathcal{C}_1$ can usually be shown to contain a set that is immune to $\mathcal{C}_2$.

Somewhat surprisingly, it seems that it will represent a significant breakthrough if one is able to present a language in P (or even in NP) that is immune to AC^0 (or to show that no such language exists). As we show below, these questions are very closely related to questions about the complexity of sets in E.

Note that if L is a P-printable set, then L is accepted by a family of constant-depth circuits of unbounded fan-in AND and OR gates $\{C_n\}$ where the function $n \mapsto C_n$ is computable in polynomial time. Call the set of languages accepted by circuits of this type P-Uniform AC^0. It is not known if P-Uniform $AC^0 = AC^0$; the P-uniformity condition just described is much less restrictive than the uniformity condition of [BIS90]. This is addressed by the following theorem:

Theorem 14. [AG91] *P-Uniform $AC^0 = AC^0$ iff $E = \bigcup_k \Sigma_k time(n)$.*[10]

This may be taken as evidence that AC^0 is properly contained in P-uniform AC^0, because $E = \bigcup_k \Sigma_k time(n)$ implies that $E = \text{DSPACE}(n) = \text{NSPACE}(n)$, as well as implying that the polynomial hierarchy collapses and is equal to PSPACE (which in turn is equal to $\text{DTIME}(2^{n^{O(1)}})$).

Recall that every NE predicate is solvable in exponential time if and only if every set in NP has an infinite P-printable subset. By the observations in the preceding paragraph, this happens only if every set in NP has an infinite subset in P-Uniform AC^0. Thus we observe:

Observation 15. *If every NE predicate is solvable in exponential time and $E = \bigcup_k \Sigma_k time(n)$, then no set in NP is immune to AC^0.*

The hypothesis of this observation seems quite unlikely; $\bigcup_k \Sigma_k time(n)$ appears to be a small subclass of E, and they can be equal only if the polynomial hierarchy collapses. Assuming $E = \bigcup_k \Sigma_k time(n)$ thus says that E is "not very powerful" in some sense, and it seems difficult to imagine that exponential time could simultaneously be powerful enough to solve all NE predicates. Nonetheless, it is shown in [AG91] that:

Theorem 16. [AG91] *There is an oracle relative to which all NE predicates are solvable in exponential time and $E = \bigcup_k \Sigma_k time(n)$.*

Thus it would represent a significant advance at this time to show that there *are* sets in NP that are immune to AC^0. The oracle construction in [AG91] makes heavy use of the notions of time-bounded Kolmogorov complexity surveyed here.

Conversely, it was observed in [AG91] that if P=NP, then there is a set in P that is immune to AC^0 (because P=NP implies there is a set in E that is

---

[10] $\Sigma_k time(n)$ is the linear-time analog of the kth level of the polynomial-time hierarchy.

immune to $\bigcup_k \Sigma_k \text{time}(n)$, and this gives rise to a tally set in P that is immune to AC^0). Thus it will also be very significant if one can show that there are *no* sets in NP that are immune to AC^0.

6 Conclusion

We have studied one method of measuring the time-bounded Kolmogorov complexity of sets, and we have surveyed a number of applications of this measure to different topics in complexity theory. We believe that functions of the form K_L offer a useful way of visualizing the complexity of a set, and we hope that they will prove useful in more situations to come.

7 Acknowledgments

I thank Ken Regan and Jack Lutz for helpful comments regarding genericity.

References

[All85]   E. Allender. *Invertible Functions*. PhD thesis, Georgia Institute of Technology, 1985.

[All89a] E. Allender. Some consequences of the existence of pseudorandom generators. *J. Comput. System Sci.* 39:101–124, 1989.

[All89b] E. Allender. The generalized Kolmogorov complexity of sets. In *Proc. 4th IEEE Structure in Complexity Theory Conf.*, pages 186–194, 1989.

[AG91]   E. Allender and V. Gore. On strong separations from AC^0. In *Proc. Fundamentals of Computation Theory*, Springer-Verlag, Lecture Notes in Computer Science 529:1–15, 1991.

[AR88]   E. Allender and R. Rubinstein. P-printable sets. *SIAM J. Comput.* 17:1193–1202, 1988.

[AW90]   E. Allender and O. Watanabe. Kolmogorov complexity and degrees of tally sets. *Inform. and Computation* 86:160–178, 1990.

[AFH87]   K. Ambos-Spies, H. Fleischhack, and H. Huwig. Diagonalizations over polynomial-time computable sets. *Theoret. Comput. Sci.* 51:177–204, 1987.

[BGS75]   T. Baker, J. Gill, and R. Solovay. Relativizations of the P=?NP question. *SIAM J. Comput.* 4:431–444, 1975.

[BDG87]   J. Balcázar, J. Díaz, and J. Gabarró. Characterizations of the class PSPACE/poly. *Theoret. Comput. Sci.* 52:251–267, 1987.

[BG81]   C. Bennett and J. Gill. Relative to a random oracle, $P(A) \neq NP(A) \neq Co\text{-}NP(A)$ with probability 1. *SIAM J. Comput.* 10:96-113, 1981.

[BGM90]   A. Bertoni, M. Goldwurm, and P. Massazza. Counting problems and algebraic formal power series in noncommuting variables. *Inform. Processing Letters* 34:117–121, 1990.

[BGS91]   A. Bertoni, M. Goldwurm, and N. Sabadini. The complexity of computing the number of strings of given length in context-free languages. *Theoret. Comput. Sci.* 86:325–342, 1991.

[BIS90]   D. Mix Barrington, N. Immerman, and H. Straubing. On uniformity within NC^1. *J. Comput. System Sci.* 41:274–306, 1990.

[Blu67]   M. Blum. A machine-independent theory of the complexity of recursive functions. *J. ACM* 14:322–336, 1967.

[BI87]   M. Blum and R. Impagliazzo. Generic oracles and oracle classes. In *Proc. 28th IEEE Symp. Foundations of Computer Science*, pages 118–126, 1987.

[Boo91]   R. Book. Some observations on separating complexity classes. *SIAM J. Comput.* 20:246–258, 1991.

[Boo92]   R. Book. On sets with small information content. In this volume.

[BH88]   R. Boppana and R. Hirschfeld. Pseudorandom generators and complexity classes. In *Advances in Computing Research*. Volume 5: *Randomness and Computation*, pages 1–26. Edited by S. Micali. JAI Press, Greenwich, CT, 1988.

[BS90]   R. Boppana and M. Sipser. The complexity of finite functions. In *Handbook of Theoretical Computer Science*. Vol. A: *Algorithms and Complexity*, pages 757–804. Edited by J. van Leeuwen. MIT Press (in the United States, Canada, and Japan), and Elsevier Science Publishers (in other countries), 1990.

[Cai89]   J.-Y. Cai. With probability one, a random oracle separates PSPACE from the polynomial-time hierarchy. *J. Comput. System Sci.* 38:68–85, 1989.

[CGH90]   B. Chor, O. Goldreich, and J. Håstad. The random oracle hypothesis is false. Technical report 631, Department of Computer Science, Technion – Israel Institute of Technology, 1990.

[Dow82]   M. Dowd. Forcing and the P hierarchy. Technical report LCSR-TR-35, Laboratory for Computer Science Research, Rutgers University, 1982.

[Fen91]   S. Fenner. Notions of resource-bounded category and genericity. In *Proc. 6th IEEE Structure in Complexity Theory Conf.*, pages 196–212, 1991.

[Gas87]   W. Gasarch. Oracles: three new results. In *Mathematical Logic and Theoretical Computer Science*, Marcel Dekker, Inc., Lecture Notes in Pure and Applied Mathematics 106:219–251, 1987.

[GS91]   A. Goldberg and M. Sipser. Compression and ranking. *SIAM J. Comput.* 20:524–536, 1991.

[Gor90]   V. Gore. Personal communication.

[Har83]   J. Hartmanis. Generalized Kolmogorov complexity and the structure of feasible computations. In *Proc. 24th IEEE Symp. Foundations of Computer Science*, pages 439–445, 1983.

[HCRR90]   J. Hartmanis, R. Chang, D. Ranjan, and P. Rohatgi. Structural complexity theory: recent surprises. In *Proc. 2nd Scandinavian Workshop on Algorithm Theory*, Springer-Verlag, Lecture Notes in Computer Science 447:1–12, 1990.

[HH88]   J. Hartmanis and L. Hemachandra. On sparse oracles separating feasible complexity classes. *Inform. Processing Letters* 28:291–296, 1988.

[HY84]   J. Hartmanis and Y. Yesha. Computation times of NP sets of different densities. *Theoret. Comput. Sci.* 34:17–32, 1984.

[Hås86]   J. Håstad. *Computational Limitations for Small-Depth Circuits*. MIT Press, 1986.

[Hås90]   J. Håstad. Pseudo-random generators under uniform assumptions. In *Proc. 22nd ACM Symp. Theory of Computing*, pages 395–404, 1990.

[HR90]   L. Hemachandra and S. Rudich. On the complexity of ranking. *J. Comput. System Sci.* 41:251–271, 1990.

[Huy85]   D. Huynh. Non-uniform complexity and the randomness of certain complete languages. Technical report TR 85-34, Computer Science Department, Iowa State University, 1985.

[Huy86]   D. Huynh. Resource-bounded Kolmogorov complexity of hard languages. In *Proc. Structure in Complexity Theory*, Springer-Verlag, Lecture Notes in Computer Science 223:184–195, 1986.

[Huy90a]   D. Huynh. The complexity of ranking simple languages. *Math. Systems Theory* 23:1–20, 1990.

[Huy90b]   D. Huynh. Efficient detectors and constructors for simple languages. Technical report UTDCS-26-90, Computer Science Program, University of Texas at Dallas, 1990.

[IT89]   R. Impagliazzo and G. Tardos. Decision versus search in super-polynomial time. In *Proc. 30th IEEE Symp. Foundations of Computer Science*, pages 222–227, 1989.

[ILL89]   R. Impagliazzo, L. Levin, and M. Luby. Pseudo-random generation from one-way functions. In *Proc. 21st ACM Symp. Theory of Computing*, pages 12–24, 1989.

[KGY89]   M. Kharitonov, A. Goldberg, and M. Yung. Lower bounds for pseudorandom number generators. In *Proc. 30th IEEE Symp. Foundations of Computer Science*, pages 242–247, 1989.

[Ko86]   K. Ko. On the notion of infinite pseudorandom sequences. *Theoret. Comput. Sci.* 48:9–33, 1986.

[Kur83]   S. Kurtz. Notions of weak genericity. *J. Symbolic Logic* 48:764–770, 1983.

[KMR89]   S. Kurtz, S. Mahaney, and J. Royer. The isomorphism conjecture fails relative to a random oracle. In *Proc. 21st ACM Symp. Theory of Computing*, pages 157–166, 1989.

[KMR91]   S. Kurtz, S. Mahaney, and J. Royer. Average dependence and random oracles. Technical report SU-CIS-91-03, School of Computer and Information Science, Syracuse University, 1991.

[Kur83]   S. Kurtz. On the random oracle hypothesis. *Inform. and Control* 57:40–47, 1983.

[Lev73]   L. Levin. Universal sequential search problems. *Problems Inform. Transmission* 9:265–266, 1973.

[Lev84]   L. Levin. Randomness conservation inequalities; information and independence in mathematical theories. *Inform. and Control* 61:15–37, 1984.

[LV90]   M. Li and P. Vitányi. Applications of Kolmogorov complexity in the theory of computation. In *Complexity Theory Retrospective*, pages 147–203. Edited by A. Selman. Springer-Verlag, 1990.

[Lut90]   J. Lutz. Category and measure in complexity classes. *SIAM J. Comput.* 19:1100–1131, 1990.

[Lut91]   J. Lutz. Almost everywhere high nonuniform complexity. *J. Comput. System Sci.*, to appear. A preliminary version appeared in *Proc. 4th IEEE Structure in Complexity Theory Conf.*, pages 37–53, 1989.

[Maa82]   W. Maass. Recursively enumerable generic sets. *J. Symbolic Logic* 47:809–823, 1982.

[Meh73]   K. Mehlhorn. On the size of sets of computable functions. In *Proc. 14th IEEE Symp. Switching and Automata Theory*, pages 190–196, 1973.

[MS90]   M. Mundhenk and R. Schuler. Non-uniform complexity classes and random languages. In *Proc. 5th IEEE Structure in Complexity Theory Conf.*, pages 110–119, 1990.

[Oxt80]   J. Oxtoby. *Measure and Category* (second edition). Springer-Verlag, 1980.

[Poi86]   B. Poizat. Q = NQ? *J. Symbolic Logic* 51:22–32, 1986.

[SF90]   L. Sanchis and M. Fulk. On the efficient generation of language instances. *SIAM J. Comput.* 19:281–296, 1990.

[Sip83]   M. Sipser. A complexity theoretic approach to randomness. In *Proc. 15th ACM Symp. Theory of Computing*, pages 330–335, 1983.

[Yao82]   A. Yao. Theory and applications of trapdoor functions. In *Proc. 23rd IEEE Symp. Foundations of Computer Science*, pages 80–91, 1982.

On Sets with Small Information Content [*]

Ronald V. Book

Department of Mathematics
University of California
Santa Barbara, CA 93106, USA
book%henri@hub.ucsb.edu

Abstract. The purpose of this paper is to review and summarize a number of results relating to sets with small information content such as sets with small generalized Kolmogorov complexity. The emphasis is on the role of such sets as oracle sets in the context of structural complexity theory

1 Introduction

Many of the issues that dominate the effort in computational complexity theory stem from the open problem of whether every problem solvable nondeterministically in polynomial time is in fact tractable, i.e., does P equal NP? One of the themes that has received a great deal of attention in this context is the study of the computational complexity of relativized computation, that is, the complexity of computation relative to oracle sets. It is in this area where the idea of sets with "small information content" has arisen and where many interesting results have been obtained by considering the notion of sets with "small generalized Kolmogorov complexity" and related concepts. The purpose of this paper is to review some of the recent work on these topics within structural complexity theory (see [BDG88, 90]) in order to make it known to researchers who are interested in the abundance of ideas stemming from the basic definitions of Kolmogorov complexity.

How does one measure the amount of information encoded in a set of strings? One method of doing this is to identify this notion with the inherent computational complexity of the characteristic function of the set as measured by some dynamic measure of the complexity of algorithms for computing the characteristic function, e.g., running time or amount of work space used. Thus a set that can be recognized in exponential time but not polynomial time is considered to encode more information than a set that can be recognized in polynomial time. A second method of doing this is to consider a function that bounds the "generalized Kolmogorov complexity" of the strings in the set. Then a set with large generalized Kolmogorov complexity is considered to encode more information than a

---

[*] Preparation of this paper was supported in part by the National Science Foundation under Grant CCR89–13584 and by the Alexander von Humboldt-Stiftung while the author was visiting the Institut für Informatik, TU München, Germany.

set with small generalized Kolmogorov complexity. A third method is to consider the set as an oracle set and apply operators that correspond to resource-bounded reducibilities; for example, when studying sets in the polynomial-time hierarchy, it is natural to use the "NP( )-operator": if $\mathrm{NP}(A) = \Sigma_2^{\mathrm{P}}$ but $\mathrm{NP}(B) = \Sigma_3^{\mathrm{P}}$, then B is considered to encode more information than A (since there is strong feeling that $\Sigma_2^{\mathrm{P}} \neq \Sigma_3^{\mathrm{P}}$). One of the themes of research in this area is to explore the possible relationships among these last two methods and this is what is emphasized in the present paper.

When studying structural complexity theory it is often desirable to have intrinsic characterizations of complexity classes, that is, to describe membership in the class in terms that do not involve the same concepts used in defining the class. On the one hand, such characterizations are useful in recognizing members of the class; on the other hand, they are helpful in studying properties of the class. The same theme arises in the study of sets with small information content and some intrinsic characterizations of the various classes of sets with small information content will be described.

There are many uses of the ideas surrounding the basic definition of Kolmogorov complexity in computational complexity theory. The forthcoming book by Li and Vitanyi (see [LV90]) contains a great deal of information. The purpose of the present paper is to review some of the aspects of structural complexity theory where the study of sets of strings with either high or low generalized Kolmogorov complexity is of use. There are many topics that are not covered; of particular interest in the present context is the work of Watanabe [Wat87] in his study on complete sets with respect to different polynomial time reducibilities for the class DEXT of sets recognized in time $2^{O(n)}$, the work of Allender [All89] in his study of upwards separation results, and the work of Huynh [Huy87] who uses such sets in studying the notion of a "complexity core" relative to the class of sets with polynomial-size circuits.

Section 2 contains notation and a review of some concepts of computational complexity theory and, more specifically, structural complexity theory. The idea of sets with small generalized Kolmogorov complexity is reviewed in Sect. 3, properties of this class are described, and the relationship between this class and other classes of sets with small information content is developed. In structural complexity theory, reducibilities computed with restricted computational resources, particularly those computed in polynomial time, have been the subject of much effort. In Sect. 4 some results regarding classes of sets polynomial time reducible to the sets with small generalized Kolmogorov complexity are reviewed. This review is continued in Sect. 5 where a decomposition of the class of sets with polynomial-size circuits is considered. In Sect. 6, results having to do with "lowness" are described, while in Sect. 7 characterizations of complexity classes in terms of reducibilities is reviewed.

2 Notation and Concepts from Complexity Theory

In this section notation is established and some definitions and important concepts of structural complexity are reviewed.

A fixed finite alphabet Σ is assumed and $\{0,1\} \subseteq \Sigma$. The set of all (finite) strings over Σ is denoted by Σ^*. The length of a string x will be denoted by $|x|$. The cardinality of a set S will be denoted by $\| S \|$.

A fixed polynomial time computable bijection $\langle \ , \ \rangle : \Sigma^* \times \Sigma^* \to \Sigma^*$ is assumed; such a function is a "pairing function," and it is assumed that the appropriate inverses are also computable in polynomial time.

For sets $A, B \subseteq \Sigma^*$, the *join* of A and B, $A \oplus B$, is defined to be the set $\{0x, 1y \mid x \in A, \ y \in B\}$.

For any class C of subsets of Σ^*, co-C $= \{\Sigma^* - L \mid L \in C\}$.

A *tally* set is a set of strings over a one letter alphabet (so that a tally set encodes a set of natural numbers by using unary notation). A set A is *sparse* if there is a polynomial p such that for every $n > 0$, $\| \{x \in A \mid \ |x| \leq n\} \| \leq p(n)$.

Clearly, every tally set is sparse but there are sparse sets that are not tally sets.

It is assumed that the reader is familiar with the basic ideas underlying formal models of computation and the basic issues surrounding the study of algorithms and complexity theory. Since this paper presents an overview, no specific model of computation is assumed but results are described in terms of Turing machines.

A "good" algorithm is one for which there is a fixed polynomial that serves as an upper bound to the algorithm's running time; running time is measured in terms of the size of the input, e.g., the length of the input string, so that the polynomial bound is evaluated on the size of the input. A problem is "tractable" if there is a good algorithm that solves all instances of the problem. Thus, class P of problems solvable in polynomial time is the collection of (suitable encodings of) all tractable problems.

Algorithms are "deterministic" in the sense that at any point in a computation there is at most one instruction to be executed at the next step. But there is a mathematical construct that allows there to be a choice among finitely many instructions that might be executed at the next step. This construct is called "nondeterminism" and in the case of time-bounded computation it formalizes the notion of "guessing" which instruction to perform at each step.

The class NP is the collection of (suitable encodings of) all problems that can be solved nondeterministically in polynomial time. The class NP can be characterized as follows: $A \in$ NP if and only if there exists a set $B \in$ P and a polynomial q such that $(\forall x)[x \in A \Leftrightarrow (\exists y)(|y| \leq q(|x|)$ and $\langle x, y \rangle \in B)]$; here, y is a "guess" and a polynomial-time algorithm testing membership in the set B is considered to be a "checking" procedure.

The major open problem of computational complexity theory (or even, all of computer science) is whether the classes P and NP are the same. The reader is referred to the book by Garey and Johnson [GJ79] for a description aimed at those who do not specialize in theoretical computer science, and to the books by Balcázar, Díaz, and Gabarró [BDG88, 90] for a presentation of some of the central issues of structural complexity theory.

In addition to the question of whether P and NP are equal, the question of whether NP is closed under complementation (i.e., is NP equal to co-NP?) is open.

One approach to the open problems about complexity classes is the method of relativization as used in recursive function theory. In the midst of a computation, it is sometimes desirable to obtain information from an external source; such a source is called an "oracle" and machines that utilize an oracle are "oracle machines."

An *oracle* machine is a Turing machine with a distinguished work tape and three distinguished states, $QUERY$, YES, and NO. At some step of a computation on an input string x, the machine may enter the state $QUERY$. In state $QUERY$, the machine transfers into the state YES if the string currently on the query tape is in some *oracle set* A; otherwise, the machine transfers into state NO; in either case, the query tape is instantly erased. The set of strings accepted by an oracle machine M relative to the oracle set A is $L(M, A) = \{x \mid$ there is an accepting computation of M on input x when the oracle set is $A\}$.

Oracle machines may be deterministic or nondeterministic. An oracle machine may operate within some time bound T, where T is a function of the length of the input string, and the notion of time bound for an oracle machine is just the same as that for an ordinary Turing machine. For any time bound T and oracle set A, $\mathrm{DTIME}(T, A) = \{L(M, A) \mid M$ is a deterministic oracle machine that operates within time bound $T\}$ and $\mathrm{NTIME}(T, A) = \{L(M, A) \mid M$ is a nondeterministic oracle machine that operates within time bound $T\}$. Of particular interest are the classes $\mathrm{P}(A)$ and $\mathrm{NP}(A)$ for arbitrary oracle sets A. Here $\mathrm{P}(A) = \{L(M, A) \mid M$ is a deterministic oracle machine that operates in time $p(n)$ for some fixed polynomial $p\}$, so that $\mathrm{P}(A) = \cup_{k>0}\mathrm{DTIME}(n^k, A)$. If $B \in \mathrm{P}(A)$, then we say that B is recognized in polynomial time *relative to A*.

Oracle machines are used to define Turing reducibilities that are computed within time bounds or space bounds. Thus, set A is *Turing reducible to* set B *in polynomial time*, written $A \leq_{\mathrm{T}}^{\mathrm{P}} B$, if $A \in P(B)$.

It is clear that $\leq_{\mathrm{T}}^{\mathrm{P}}$ is reflexive and transitive. For any class C of sets, define $\mathrm{P(C)} = \cup\{\mathrm{P}(A) \mid A \in \mathrm{C}\}$.

The analogous notions are used in defining $\mathrm{NP}(A)$. However, the reducibility $\leq_{\mathrm{T}}^{\mathrm{NP}}$ is not transitive. (For, if from some A, $\mathrm{NP}(A) = \mathrm{NP}(\mathrm{NP}(A))$, then co-$\mathrm{NP}(A) = \mathrm{NP}(A)$. But it is known [BGS75] that there exists a set B such that $\mathrm{NP}(B) \neq \mathrm{co\text{-}NP}(B)$.)

In addition, an oracle machine may operate within some space bound S, where S is a function of the length of the input string; in this case, it is required that the query tape as well as the ordinary work tapes be bounded in length by S. For any space bound S and oracle set A, $\mathrm{DSPACE}(S, A) = \{L(M, A) \mid M$ is a deterministic oracle machine that operates within space bound $S\}$ and $\mathrm{NSPACE}(S, A) = \{L(M, A) \mid M$ is a nondeterministic oracle machine that operates within space bound $S\}$. It is known that for appropriate space bounds S, $\mathrm{NSPACE}(S) \subseteq \mathrm{DSPACE}(S^2)$; this result also applies to classes specified by oracle machines. Thus, for arbitrary oracle sets A, $\mathrm{PSPACE}(A) = \{L(M, A) \mid M$ is a deterministic oracle machine that operates in space $p(n)$ for some fixed polynomial $p\} = \{L(M, A) \mid M$ is a nondeterministic oracle machine that operates in space $p(n)$ for some fixed polynomial $p\}$ since $\cup_{k>0}\mathrm{DSPACE}(n^k, A) = \cup_{k>0}\mathrm{NSPACE}(n^k, A)$.

There are some important complexity classes that we can now define.

Let A be a set. Define $\Sigma_0^P(A) = P(A)$, $\Sigma_1^P(A) = NP(A)$, and $\Sigma_{k+1}^P(A) = NP(\Sigma_k^P(A)) = \{L(M, A) \mid M$ is a nondeterministic oracle machine that runs in polynomial time and $A \in \Sigma_k^P(A)\}$. Define $\Delta_0^P(A) = \Delta_1^P(A) = P(A)$ and $\Delta_{k+1}^P(A) = P(\Sigma_k^P(A))$. For each i, define $\Pi_k^P(A) = \text{co-}\Sigma_k^P(A)$. Then $\Sigma_0^P(A) \subseteq \Sigma_1^P(A) \subseteq \ldots \subseteq \Sigma_k^P(A) \subseteq \ldots$ is the *polynomial-time hierarchy relative to A*, and $\Sigma_0^P \subseteq \Sigma_1^P \subseteq \ldots \subseteq \Sigma_k^P \subseteq \ldots$ is the *polynomial-time hierarchy*. Let $PH(A) = \cup_{k \geq 0} \Sigma_k^P(A)$ and $PH = \cup_{k \geq 0} \Sigma_k^P$. It is clear that for every set A, $PH(A) \subseteq PSPACE(A)$. It is not known whether the polynomial-time hierarchy extends beyond $\Sigma_0^P = P$.

There is another important type of reducibility.

Define the binary relation $\leq_m^P$ between subsets of Σ^* by $A \leq_m^P B$ if there is a function f that is computable in polynomial time and has the property that $(\forall x)(x \in A \Leftrightarrow f(x) \in B)$, i.e., $A = f^{-1}(B)$. We say that "A is many-one reducible to B in polynomial time" when $A \leq_m^P B$. For a class C of subsets of Σ^*, a set B is $\leq_m^P$-*complete* for C if $B \in$ C and for every $A \in$ C, $A \leq_m^P B$. A set that is $\leq_m^P$-complete for NP is NP-*complete*.

If $\leq_r^P$ is a reducibility computed in polynomial-time, then a set B is $\leq_r^P$-*hard* for NP if there is an NP-complete set A such that $A \leq_r^P B$.

Define $A \equiv_m^P B$ if $A \leq_m^P B$ and $B \leq_m^P A$; A and B are said to be *many-one equivalent* in polynomial time. Similarly, define $A \equiv_T^P B$ if $A \leq_T^P B$ and $B \leq_T^P A$; A and B are said to be *Turing equivalent* in polynomial time.

3 Sets with Small Information Content

The idea of the Kolmogorov complexity of finite strings provides one possible definition of the "degree of randomness" of a string. Informally, the Kolmogorov complexity of a finite string is the length of the shortest program that will generate the string; intuitively, it is a measure of the amount of information that the string contains. A string is considered to be "random" if the length of the shortest problem that generates the string is the same as that of the string itself. This concept has been studied extensively; recently, it has found many applications in computer science and, particularly, in computational complexity theory (see [LV90]).

A modification of the idea of Kolmogorov complexity has also been developed: consider not only the length of a program but also, simultaneously, the running time of the program. This modification has been used by Ko [Ko86], by Sipser [Sip83], and by Hartmanis [Har83] who considered the notion of "a generalized, two-parameter Kolmogorov complexity measure for finite strings which measures how far a given string can be compressed and how easily it can be recomputed from the shortened representation": given a universal Turing machine U and functions G and g, a string x of length n is in the generalized Kolmogorov class $K_U[g(n), G(n)]$ if there is a string y of length at most $g(n)$ with the property that U will generate x on input y in at most $G(n)$ steps.

A set A of strings has *small generalized Kolmogorov complexity* if there exist constants c and k such that for almost every x, x is in A if and only if x is in $K_U[c \cdot \log n, n^k]$ where $n = |x|$. The class of sets with small generalized Kolmogorov complexity is denoted **K[log, poly]**.

Allender and Rubinstein [AR88] have provided a useful intrinsic characterization of the class **K[log, poly]**.

Theorem 1. *A set has small generalized Kolmogorov complexity if and only if it is p-isomorphic to a tally set, i.e., set S is in **K[log, poly]** if and only if there is a tally set T and a bijection f mapping S onto T such that both f and f^{-1} can be computed in polynomial time.*

Since most of the properties of sets and of classes of sets studied in computational complexity theory are invariant under p-isomorphism, Theorem 1 shows that for the purposes of complexity theory, *the class of tally sets can be identified, up to p-isomorphism, with the class of sets with small generalized Kolmogorov complexity*. This means that the properties of the class of tally sets (a very well-studied class) are of interest with considering sets with small information content.

For any arbitrary set $A \subseteq \{0,1\}^*$, there is a tally set T_A that represents the unary encodings of the strings in A when those strings are viewed as integers encoded in binary. It is easy to see that $T_A \leq_{\mathrm{m}}^{\mathrm{P}} A$ and that there is a function f computable in exponential time that computes a bijection from A to T_A. From Theorem 1, one sees that this fact implies the existence of sets of small generalized Kolmogorov complexity that are arbitrarily complex when the inherent computational complexity is measured by the running time or work space or any of the other standard dynamic measures (which are recursively related). Since the inherent computational complexity of a set has meaning only when the set is recursive, this fact implies that there is no possibility of finding a relationship between the inherent computational complexity of a set and a bound on the generalized Kolmogorov complexity of that same set.

In the remainder of this section, properties of the class **K[log, poly]** are investigated by using the interpretation based on Theorem 1. This leads to the investigation of other classes of sets that have properties that are generalizations of properties of the class of tally sets.

For any set A, let $enum_A$ be the function, that for each string 0^n, has value a string encoding the set of all strings in A of length at most n. Set A is *self-p-printable* if there is a deterministic oracle Turing machine that computes relative to A the function $enum_A$ and that runs in polynomial time.

Notice that every self-p-printable set is sparse. It is easy to see that $\mathrm{P} = \mathrm{NP}$ if and only if for every self-p-printable set A, $\mathrm{P}(A) = \mathrm{NP}(A)$. Hartmanis and Hemachandra [HH88] have shown that the class of self-p-printable sets can be viewed as a relativized version of **K[log, poly]**.

Theorem 2. *A set A is self-p-printable if and only if $A \in \mathbf{K}^{\mathbf{A}}[\mathbf{log}, \mathbf{poly}]$, that is, there is a universal oracle machine U and constants c and k with the property* *that for almost every x, x is in A if and only if x is in $\mathrm{K}_{UA}[c \cdot \log n,\ n^k]$ where $n = |x|$.*

The idea of a "self-p-printable set" is easily generalized. For sets A and B, A is *P(B)-printable* if there is a deterministic oracle machine that computes relative to B the function $enum_A$ and that runs in polynomial time. Clearly, if A is $\mathrm{P}(B)$-printable, then A is sparse.

The reader should also consider the results of Allender and Rubinstein [AR88] considering the printability of sets.

A class that plays an important role in the discussion of sets with small information content is the class of sets with "polynomial-size circuits."

Let $A \subseteq \{0,1\}^*$. If $\mathbf{C}_A = \{C_n\}_{n>0}$ is a family of Boolean circuits (i.e., circuits with 'and', 'or', and 'not' gates) such that for every $n > 0$, C_n computes the characteristic function of $\{x \in A \mid\ |x|\ \leq n\}$, then $\mathbf{C}_A$ *recognizes* A. If there is a function f such that for every C_n in $\mathbf{C}_A$, the size of C_n is bounded above by $f(n)$ (where the size of C_n is the number of gates in C_n), then A has $f(n)$-*size circuits*.

It is easy to see that every set $A \subseteq \{0,1\}^*$ has exponential-size circuits. The class of interest is the class of sets with polynomial-size circuits, i.e., the class of sets A such that there is a family $\mathbf{C}_A = \{C_n\}_{n>0}$ of circuits that recognizes A and has the property that for some polynomial p and all $n > 0$, the size of C_n is bounded above by $p(n)$. Clearly, every sparse set has polynomial-size circuits so there are sets that are not recursive but do have polynomial-size circuits. On the other hand, there are recursive sets that do not have polynomial-size circuits [Kan82].

The class P/poly is the collection of all sets A such that there exists a polynomial length-bounded function $h : \{0\}^* \rightarrow \{0,1\}^*$ and a set $B \in \mathrm{P}$ with the property that for every $x \in \{0,1\}^*$, $x \in A$ if and only if $\langle x, h(0^{|x|}) \rangle \in B$.

Theorem 3. *For any set $A \subseteq \{0,1\}^*$, the following are equivalent.*

(a) *A has polynomial-size circuits;*
(b) *A is in* P/poly;
(c) *there is a sparse set S such that A is Turing reducible in polynomial time to S;*
(d) *there is a tally set T such that A is Turing reducible in polynomial time to T.*

Corollary 4. *For any set $A \subseteq \{0,1\}^*$, A has polynomial-size circuits if and only if there is a set S with small generalized Kolmogorov complexity such that A is Turing reducible to S in polynomial time.*

Pippenger [Pip79] showed the equivalence of (a) and (b). The equivalence of (a) and (c) is attributed to A. Meyer in [BH77]. The equivalence of (c) and (d) has been proved in several places; see [BDG88]. The corollary follows by combining Theorem 1 and Theorem 3.

Because of Theorem 3, the class of sets with polynomial-size circuits is denoted by P/poly.

An interesting subclass of P/poly is the class of sets with "self-producible" circuits studied by Ko[Ko85].

Set A has *self-producible circuits* if there exists a polynomial length-bounded function $h : \{0\}^* \rightarrow \{0,1\}^*$ and a set $B \in$ P with the properties that (i) for every $x \in \{0,1\}^*$, $x \in A$ if and only if $\langle x, h(0^{|x|})\rangle \in B$, and (ii) h can be computed relative to A by a deterministic polynomial time-bounded oracle transducer.

Balcázar and Book [BB86] have provided an intrinsic characterization of the class of sets with self-producible circuits that is similar to the characterization of the class **K[log, poly]**.

Theorem 5. *A set has self-producible circuits if and only if it is polynomial-time Turing equivalent to a tally set (i.e., $A \leq_T^P T$ and $T \leq_T^P A$).*

The characterizations in both Theorem 1 and Theorem 5 depend on the class of tally sets. The difference between the two characterizations is in the type of reducibility that is used. The former case uses p-isomorphisms and the latter case uses polynomial-time Turing equivalence. These are very different notions in general and are different when applied to the class of tally sets (as will be seen in the next section).

The relationships between three of the classes defined so far was shown by Balcázar and Book.

Theorem 6.

(a) *Every set with small generalized Kolmogorov complexity is self-p-printable, but there are sparse sets that are self-p-printable but do not have small generalized Kolmogorov complexity.*

(b) *Every self-p-printable set has self-producible circuits, but there are sets that have self-producible circuits but are not self-p-printable.*

It is known that there are nonsparse sets that have self-producible circuits and such sets cannot be self-p-printable (since they are not sparse). Shou-wen Tang (personal communication) has shown that if there is a sparse set that has self-producible circuits but is not self-p-printable, then P $\neq$ NP.

In the context of Theorems 1, 3, and 6, other classes of sets are of interest. Their definitions stem from the problem of determining the inherent computational complexity of the characteristic function of sets.

For an oracle machine M, a set A, and a string x, let $Q(M, A, x) = \{y \mid$ there is a computation of M on x relative to A that queries the oracle about y's membership in $A\}$. For every set A, let $\mathrm{NP}_B(A) = \{L(M, A) \mid$ there is a polynomial q such that for all x, $\| Q(M, A, x) \| \leq q(|x|)\}$.

Let SAT denote the set of Boolean formulas in conjunctive normal form that are satisfiable. Recall that SAT is the first NP-complete set. (For the purposes of the present paper, SAT could denote any NP-complete set.)

Book, Long, and Selman [BLS84] showed (i) for every set A, P$(A) \subseteq \mathrm{NP}_B(A)$ $\subseteq$ P$(A \oplus SAT)$, (ii) P $=$ NP if and only if for every set A, P$(A) = \mathrm{NP}_B(A)$ if and only if for every set A, $SAT \in$ P(A) if and only if for every set A,

$P(A) = P(A \oplus SAT)$, and (iii) NP = co-NP if and only if for every set A, $NP_B(A) = \text{co-NP}_B(A)$ if and only if for every set A, $\overline{SAT} \in NP_B(A)$ if and only if for every set A, $NP_B(A) = P(A \oplus SAT)$.

If a set A has the property that $NP(A) = NP_B(A)$, then the set A does not encode a great deal of information since it can be retrieved by using the $NP_B(\ )$ operator which forces a strong restriction on access to the oracle. For example, if $NP(SAT) = NP_B(SAT)$, then $\Sigma_2^P = \Delta_2^P$ so that the polynomial-time hierarchy extends no further than Δ_2^P.

If a set A has self-producible circuits, then $NP(A) = NP_B(A)$ so $NP(A) \subseteq P(A \oplus SAT)$. However, there are sets with this property that do not have self-producible circuits.

Theorem 7. *There is a set A such that* $P(A) = NP_B(A) = NP(A) = P(A \oplus SAT)$ *and A does not have polynomial size-circuits and, hence, does not have self-producible circuits.*

Proof. Let A be any set that is $\leq_T^P$-complete for EXPSPACE. (Recall that EXPSPACE $= \text{DSPACE}(2^{poly})$.) If A has polynomial-size circuits, then there exists a sparse set S such that $A \leq_T^P S$. Since A is $\leq_T^P$-complete for EXPSPACE, it is the case that for every set $B \in$ EXPSPACE, $B \leq_T^P A$ so that $A \leq_T^P S$ implies $B \leq_T^P S$. Thus, by Theorem 3, every set in EXPSPACE has polynomial-size circuits. But Kannan [Kan82] showed there are sets in EXPSPACE that do not have polynomial-size circuits. Hence, A does not have polynomial-size circuits.

Since A is $\leq_T^P$-complete for EXPSPACE, $SAT \in$ EXPSPACE, and $P(\text{EXPSPACE}) = NP(\text{EXPSPACE}) = \text{EXPSPACE}$, it follows that $P(A) = NP_B(A) = NP(A) = P(A \oplus SAT)$.

In a different context, Kurtz [Kur83] showed that with probability one, for a randomly selected set A, $NP(A) \not\subseteq P(A \oplus SAT)$. From this one can show that with probability one, for a randomly selected set A, $NP_B(A) \neq NP(A)$ (see [Boo91].)

Since for every set A, $NP_B(A) \subseteq NP(A)$ and $NP_B(A) \subseteq P(A \oplus SAT)$, it is of interest to compare the classes discussed above with the class $\{A \mid NP(A) = NP_B(A)\}$ and the class $\{A \mid NP(A) \subseteq P(A \oplus SAT)\}$. The first of these classes is included in the second and from the last paragraph one can see that with probability one, a randomly selected set is not in the latter class. If the polynomial-time hierarchy extends properly up to at least Σ_2^P, that is, $\Delta_2^P \neq \Sigma_2^P$, then a candidate for a specific example is SAT since $NP(SAT) = \Sigma_2^P$, $P(SAT \oplus SAT) = P(SAT) = \Delta_2^P$, and $\Delta_2^P \neq \Sigma_2^P$ implies that $NP_B(SAT) \neq NP(SAT)$ (since $\Delta_2^P = P(SAT) \subseteq NP_B(SAT) \subseteq P(SAT \oplus SAT) = \Delta_2^P$).

If one considers other bounds on the generalized Kolmogorov complexity of sets, do similar properties hold? Does the information that $NP(A) \subseteq P(A \oplus SAT)$ yield any information about the generalized Kolmogorov complexity of A? It is likely that the answer to the last question is "no," since any set that is $\leq_T^P$-complete (or $\leq_m^P$-complete) for EXPSPACE has this property and has high generalized Kolmogorov complexity.

The reader should note that if C is a class of sets such that for every $A \in C$, $NP_B(A) = NP(A)$, then showing the existence of a set $A \in C$ such that $P(A) \neq NP(A)$ is equivalent to showing that $P \neq NP$. Similarly, if C is a class of sets such that for every $A \in C$, $NP(A) \subseteq P(A \oplus SAT)$, then showing the existence of a set $A \in C$ such that $NP(A) \neq P(A \oplus SAT)$ is equivalent to showing that $NP \neq co\text{-}NP$ since it shows the existence of a set A such that $NP_B(A) \neq P(A \oplus SAT)$. Thus, the classification of sets A as to whether $NP(A) = NP_B(A)$ or whether $NP(A) \subseteq P(A \oplus SAT)$ has merit. The class of sets with self-producible circuits is an example of such a class C and it is the largest known class having those properties and being defined in a way that those properties are not themselves used. It is of considerable interest to identify the largest class having those properties and being defined in a way that those properties are not themselves used. Long [Lon85] has shown that there exists a recursive sparse set S such that $NP_B(S) \neq NP(S)$; for this S, $P(S) \neq NP(S)$ and S does not have self-producible circuits. In addition, Long showed that for every sparse set S_1, there exists a sparse set S_2 such that $NP(S_1) \subseteq NP_B(S_2)$. Allender and Hemachandra [AH89] showed the existence of a sparse set S such that $NP(S) \not\subseteq P(S \oplus SAT)$.

There has been a great deal of effort expended in the construction of sets that when used as oracle sets result in the separation or collapse of various relativized complexity classes. For example, there exist sets A and B such that $P(A) = NP(A)$ and $P(B) \neq NP(B)$, but for almost every set C, $P(C) \neq NP(C)$. What happens if the oracle set is required to be a set with small generalized Kolmogorov complexity? Using the characterization of sets with small generalized Kolmogorov complexity as being p-isomorphic to tally sets, one can see that the situation is different, as shown by Long and Selman [LS86].

Theorem 8.

(a) $P \neq NP$ *if and only if there exists a set A with small generalized Kolmogorov complexity such that $P(A) \neq NP(A)$.*

(b) $NP \neq co\text{-}NP$ *if and only if there exists a set A with small generalized Kolmogorov complexity such that $NP(A) \neq co\text{-}NP(A)$.*

Combining Theorem 8 with the characterization of sets with self-producible circuits (and simple properties of reducibilities), one obtains the following fact.

Corollary 9.

(a) $P \neq NP$ *if and only if there exists a set A with self-producible circuits such that $P(A) \neq NP(A)$.*

(b) $NP \neq co\text{-}NP$ *if and only if there exists a set A with self-producible circuits such that $NP(A) \neq co\text{-}NP(A)$.*

4 Using Reducibilities to Obtain Information

Consider another approach to the problem of defining the amount of information encoded in a set of strings: the set is considered as an oracle set and operators corresponding to various resource-bounded reducibilities are applied. In Sect. 3, the type of reducibility considered was Turing reducibility (or some modification of it). But there are circumstances where less computational power is needed to compute the reducibility and, hence, to obtain the information encoded in a set. In Sect. 2, just two types of reducibilities were described, many-one ($\leq_m^P$) and Turing ($\leq_T^P$). But there are other reducibilities that are studied in complexity theory and results about these reducibilities help illustrate this. Some of this material is described in this section.

If f is a function that witnesses $A\leq_m^P B$, then for each x, the question "is $f(x)$ in B?" is asked just once. If M is an oracle machine that witnesses $A\leq_T^P B$, then for any x, the computation of M on x relative to B may ask whether a computed query string is in B for as many query strings as are generated in the computation and, in general, this number is bounded only by the number of steps in the computation. Thus, when one considers different notions of reducibilities, one property of interest is the number of questions that are allowed in any given computation. It turns out that there are infinitely many polynomial-time reducibilities that lie between many-one and Turing.

Turing reducibility has the property that the answer to one query may influence the generation of the next query string. This means that this type of reducibility is "adaptive". The idea of "non-adaptive" reducibilities is captured by the notion of "truth-table" reducibility where all the query strings are generated before any of the oracle queries are made.

Define reducibilities computed in polynomial time as follows:

(i) for every $k > 0$, set A is *k-truth-table reducible* to set B, written $A\leq_{k\text{-tt}}^P B$, if there exist polynomial time computable functions f and g such that for all x, $f(x)$ is a list of k strings, $g(x)$ describes a boolean circuit with k inputs, and $x \in A$ if and only if the circuit given by $g(x)$ evaluates to true on the k-tuple $\langle \chi_B(y_1), \ldots, \chi_B(y_k) \rangle$ where $f(x) = \langle y_1, \ldots, y_k \rangle$ and χ_B is the characteristic function of B;

(ii) set A is *bounded truth-table reducible* to set B, written $A\leq_{btt}^P B$, if there is an integer k such that $A\leq_{k\text{-tt}}^P B$;

(iii) set A is *truth-table reducible* to set B, written $A\leq_{tt}^P B$ if there exist polynomial time computable functions f and g such that for all x, $f(x)$ is a list of strings, $g(x)$ is a truth-table with the number of variables being equal to the number of strings in the list $f(x)$, and $x \in A$ if and only if the truth-table $g(x)$ evaluates to true on $\langle \chi_B(y_1), \ldots, \chi_B(y_k) \rangle$ where $f(x) = \langle y_1, \ldots, y_k \rangle$.

(For properties of these reducibilities, see [LLS75].)

What is important to notice is that truth-table reducibilities are non-adaptive, that is, the list of query strings is computed before any evaluations are made so that the $i + 1^{st}$ string on the list does not depend on whether any of the first i strings on the list happen to be in the oracle set.

There are several interesting results about sets that may be reducible to sparse sets.

Theorem 10.

(a) *[OW91] If there is a sparse set that is $\leq_{btt}^{P}$-hard for NP, then P = NP.*

(b) *[KL82] If there is a sparse set that is $\leq_{T}^{P}$-hard for NP, then the polynomial-time hierarchy collapses to Σ_2^P.*

(c) *[OL91] If there is a sparse set that is $\leq_{btt}^{P}$-hard for PSPACE, then P = PSPACE.*

(d) *[KL82] If there is a sparse set that is $\leq_{T}^{P}$-hard for PSPACE, then PSPACE = Σ_2^P.*

(e) *[BBS86a] The polynomial-time hierarchy collapses if and only if for every sparse set S, the polynomial-time hierarchy relative to S collapses if and only if there exists a sparse set S such that the polynomial-time hierarchy relative to S collapses.*

(f) *[BBS86a] The union of the classes in the polynomial-time hierarchy is equal to PSPACE if and only if for every sparse set S, the union of the classes in the polynomial-time hierarchy relative to S is equal to PSPACE relative to S if and only if there exists a sparse set S such that the union of the classes in the polynomial-time hierarchy relative to S is equal to PSPACE relative to S.*

Most researchers in the field believe that the polynomial-time hierarchy extends to infinitely many levels. The results in Theorem 10 suggest that the information encoded in a sparse set is not powerful enough to force a collapse of the hierarchy even if a powerful computational operator is used to retrieve that information.

In contrast, consider the *algorithmically random* sets of Martin-Löf [Mar66], sets that encode a great deal of information. It has been shown recently [BLW92] that even with a powerful computational operator, it may be extremely difficult to retrieve that information. This is illustrated by the following result.

Theorem 11.

(a) *If there exists an algorithmically random set that is $\leq_{btt}^{P}$-hard for NP, then P = NP.*

(b) *If there exists an algorithmically random set that is $\leq_{btt}^{P}$-hard for PSPACE, then P = PSPACE.*

(c) *If there exists an algorithmically random set that is $\leq_{T}^{P}$-hard for NP, then the polynomial-time hierarchy collapses.*

(d) *If there exists an algorithmically random set that is $\leq_{T}^{P}$-hard for PSPACE, then PH=PSPACE.*

5 A Decomposition of P/poly

Since Theorem 1 essentially identifies the sets with small generalized Kolmogorov complexity with the class of tally sets, certain results about the class of sets with polynomial-size circuits are of interest. Recall from Theorem 3 that a set has polynomial-size circuits if and only if it is Turing reducible in polynomial time to some tally set. Some results about sets reducible to tally sets by means of these reducibilities will be reviewed here.

Recall that truth-table reducibilities are non-adaptive, that is, the list of query strings is computed before any evaluations are made so that the $i + 1^{st}$ string on the list does not depend on whether any of the first i strings on the list happen to be in the oracle set.

For any reducibility r computed in polynomial time and any class $\mathbf{C}$ of sets, let $P_r(\mathbf{C}) = \{A \mid \text{there exists } C \in \mathbf{C} \text{ such that } A \leq_r^P B\}$. Also, for any truth-table reducibility r computed in polynomial time, $A \equiv_r^P B$ denotes the fact that $A \leq_r^P B$ and $B \leq_r^P A$. For any class $\mathbf{C}$ of sets, let $E_r^P(\mathbf{C})$ denote $\{A \mid \text{there exists } C \in \mathbf{C} \text{ such that } A \equiv_r^P C\}$. In addition, write $P_T(\mathbf{C})$ for $P(\mathbf{C})$. Thus, for any reducibility r and for any class $\mathbf{C}$, $E_r^P(\mathbf{C}) \subseteq P_r(\mathbf{C})$. From Theorem 3, this notation can be used to denote the class of sets with polynomial size circuits in each of the following ways: $P_T(\text{SPARSE})$, $P_T(\text{TALLY})$, $P_T(\mathbf{K[\log, poly]})$, or P/poly; and the class of sets with self-producible circuits can be denoted $E_T^P(\text{TALLY})$ or $E_T^P(\mathbf{K[\log, poly]})$.

It is clear that for any tally set T, $A \leq_T^P T$ if and only if $A \leq_{tt}^P T$. Thus, $P/\text{poly} = P_{tt}(\text{TALLY}) = P_{tt}(\mathbf{K[\log, poly]})$. What relationship do classes such as $P_{k\text{-}tt}(\text{TALLY})$ or $P_{btt}(\text{TALLY})$ have with P/poly? Book and Ko [BK88] investigated this question and obtained the following results .

Theorem 12. $P_{btt}(\text{TALLY}) = P_m(\text{TALLY})$ *and* $P_{btt}(\text{TALLY}) \neq P/\text{poly}$.

Thus, while there are infinitely many different polynomial time reducibilities, there are only two classes of the form $P_r(\text{TALLY})$, P/poly and $P_m(\text{TALLY})$. The reader must be cautioned that this should not be interpreted as saying that for every tally set T, $P_m(T) = P_{btt}(T)$; this is certainly not the case as was shown by Tang and Book [TB91].

Theorem 13.

(a) *For almost every tally set* T, $P_m(T) \neq P_{1\text{-}tt}(T)$ *and* $P_{btt}(T) \neq P_{tt}(T)$.
(b) *For every* $k > 0$ *and for almost every tally set* T, $P_{k\text{-}tt}(T) \neq P_{(k+1)\text{-}tt}(T)$.

Given the fact that $P_{tt}(\text{TALLY}) = P_T(\text{TALLY})$ and $P_m(\text{TALLY}) = P_{btt}(\text{TALLY})$, there is the question of whether the class TALLY (equivalently, $\mathbf{K[\log, poly]}$) can be used to separate the reducibilities $\leq_{tt}^P$ and $\leq_T^P$. Tang and Book [TB88] determined that this could be done if classes of the form $E_r^P(\text{TALLY})$ were considered.

Theorem 14. $E_{tt}^P(\text{TALLY}) \neq E_T^P(\text{TALLY})$ *and* $E_{btt}^P(\text{TALLY}) \neq E_{tt}^P(\text{TALLY})$.

But Tang and Book were not able to determine whether $E_{btt}^P(TALLY)$ is equal to $E_m^P(\text{TALLY})$. Based on the work of Tang and Book, Allender and Watanabe [AW88] developed a very interesting result.

Theorem 15. *Either* $E_m^P(\text{TALLY}) = E_{btt}^P(\text{TALLY})$, *or* $E_m^P(\text{TALLY}) \neq E_{1\text{-}tt}^P(\text{TALLY})$ *and for every* $k > 0$, $E_{k\text{-}tt}^P(\text{TALLY}) \neq E_{(k+1)\text{-}tt}^P(\text{TALLY})$.

Allender and Watanabe described a certain condition Q with the property that if Q is true, then $E_m^P(\text{TALLY}) = E_{btt}^P(\text{TALLY})$, and if Q is false, then $E_m^P(\text{TALLY}) \neq E_{1\text{-tt}}^P(\text{TALLY})$ and for every $k > 0$, $E_{k\text{-tt}}^P(\text{TALLY}) \neq E_{(k+1)\text{-tt}}^P(\text{TALLY})$. Condition Q is a statement about the nonexistence of a specific type of "one-way" function, and condition Q holds if and only if for every length-increasing function $f : \Sigma^* \to \{0\}^*$ computable in polynomial time, there exists a t such that for all x in the image of f, $f^{-1}(x) \cap K[t \cdot \log n, n^t] \neq \phi$ where $n = |x|$. Thus, once again sets with small generalized Kolmogorov complexity arise.

Recently, Gavalda and Watanabe [GW91] showed that no two of the following classes are equal: $E_{tt}^P(\text{SPARSE})$, $E_T^P(\text{SPARSE})$, $E_T^{SN}(\text{SPARSE})$, $E_T^{NP}(\text{SPARSE})$, where SN denotes the strong nondeterministic polynomial-time reducibility studied by Long [Lon82]. In addition, they showed $E_T^P(\text{TALLY}) \not\subseteq E_{tt}^P(\text{SPARSE})$.

6 Lowness

There is another approach to defining the amount of information encoded in a set of strings which is related to the approach discussed in Sect. 4.

One way to quantify the notion of the "power" of an oracle set is to consider notions of "lowness". The notion of lowness (from recursive function theory) was introduced in computational complexity theory by Schöning [Sch83]. In general, the notion of lowness with respect to the classes Σ_i^P, $i > 0$, may be interpreted as setting an upper bound on the amount of information that can be encoded in the set, that is, a low set in the polynomial-time hierarchy has the power of only a bounded number of alternating quantifiers or, equivalently, a bounded number of applications of the NP( )-operator. The formal definitions follow.

For $n \geq 0$, define $H_n = \{A \in \text{NP} \mid \Sigma_{n+1}^P \subseteq \Sigma_n^P(A)\}$ and $L_n = \{A \in \text{NP} \mid \Sigma_n^P(A) \subseteq \Sigma_n^P\}$. (Notice that it follows trivially from the definitions that for every set A, $\Sigma_n^P \subseteq \Sigma_n^P(A)$, and for every set $A \in \text{NP}$, $\Sigma_n^P(A) \subseteq \Sigma_{n+1}^P$.) Define $HH = \cup_{n \geq 0} H_n$ and $LH = \cup_{n \geq 0} L_n$. A set in NP is *high* if it is in HH and is *low* if it is in LH. The structure $H_0 \subseteq H_1 \subseteq H_2 \subseteq \ldots$ is the *high hierarchy* within NP and the structure $L_0 \subseteq L_1 \subseteq L_2 \subseteq \ldots$ is the *low hierarchy* within NP.

Set A is in H_n if it encodes information that is equivalent to the power of an additional application of the NP( )-operator $(\text{NP}(\Sigma_n^P) = \Sigma_{n+1}^P \subseteq \Sigma_n^P(A))$: H_0 is the class of all sets that are complete for NP with respect to polynomial-time Turing reducibilities. Set A is in L_n if continued application of the NP( )-operator yields no more than if the set were empty set $(\text{NP}(\Sigma_n^P(A)) \subseteq \text{NP}(\Sigma_n^P) = \text{NP}(\Sigma_n^P(\phi)))$; L_0 is the class P.

Some of the results (from [Sch83], [KS85]) about the high and low hierarchies within NP are given in the following:

Theorem 16.

(a) *For every $n \geq 0$, either* $L_n = H_n = \text{NP}$ *or* $L_n \cap H_n = \phi$.
(b) *For every $n \geq 0$, if* $\Sigma_n^P = \Sigma_{n+1}^P$, *then* $L_n = H_n = \text{NP}$.
(c) *For every $n \geq 0$, if* $\Sigma_n^P \neq \Sigma_{n+1}^P$, *then* $L_n \cap H_n = \phi$.

(d) *The polynomial-time hierarchy extends to infinitely many levels if and only if* $\mathrm{LH} \cap \mathrm{HH} = \phi$.

(e) *If the polynomial-time hierarchy extends to infinitely many levels, then* $\mathrm{NP} \neq \mathrm{LH} \cup \mathrm{HH}$.

(f) *Every sparse set (hence, every set with small generalized Kolmogorov complexity) in* NP *is in* L_2.

(g) *Every set in* NP *that has polynomial-size circuits is in* L_3.

While Schöning defined the notions of highness and lowness only for sets in NP, others generalized them to discuss sets in other classes. Two of those generalizations will be described briefly, the first being due to Balcázar, Book, and Schöning [BBS86b].

For every $n > 0$, define $\mathrm{EH_n} = \{A \mid \Sigma_\mathrm{n}^\mathrm{P}(A \oplus SAT) \subseteq \Sigma_\mathrm{n}^\mathrm{P}(A)\}$ and $\mathrm{EL_n} = \{A \mid \Sigma_\mathrm{n}^\mathrm{P}(A) \subseteq \Sigma_\mathrm{n-1}^\mathrm{P}(A \oplus SAT)\}$. A set is *extended high* if it belongs to $\cup_{n>0}\mathrm{EH_n}$ and is *extended low* if it belongs to $\cup_{n>0}\mathrm{LH_n}$.

Theorem 17.

1. *If a set has self-producible circuits, then it is in* EL_1; *hence, every set with small generalized Kolmogorov complexity is in* EL_1.

2. *If a set has polynomial-size circuits, then it is in* EL_3; *hence, every sparse set is in* EL_3.

3. *Either every sparse set is extended low, in which case the polynomial-time hierarchy collapses, or no sparse set is extended low, in which case the polynomial-time hierarchy extends to infinitely many levels.*

Notice that the property $\mathrm{NP}(A) \subseteq \mathrm{P}(A \oplus SAT)$ considered in Section 3 is precisely the property of being in EL_1.

Very sharp bounds on highness and lowness have been announced by Long and Sheu [LS91].

Another setting in which the notion of lowness has been investigated is that of exponential time computation. Let $\mathrm{DEXT} = \cup_{c>0}\mathrm{DTIME}(2^{cn})$.

If a set A has the property that $\mathrm{DEXT}(A) = \mathrm{DEXT}$, then A is *exponentially low*.

It is not difficult to show that if A has small generalized Kolmogorov complexity, then A is exponentially low if and only if A is in the class P. It would be interesting to classify the sparse sets that are exponentially low.

Theorem 18. *There is a sparse set that is exponentially low but is not in P.*

This result is due to Book, Orponen, Russo, and Watanabe [BORW88]. They constructed a (very) sparse set S by choosing elements of high generalized Kolmogorov complexity to put into S. In fact, $S \cap \mathrm{K}_U[n/2, 2^{3n}] = \phi$, so that no element x of S can be produced from a string of length $|x|/2$ within $2^{3|x|}$ steps and $S \notin \mathrm{P}$. But the elements are chosen such that $S \in \mathrm{DEXT}$. For any set L in $\mathrm{DEXT}(S)$, an exponential-time oracle machine M recognizing L relative to S can be simulated by an exponential time machine that does not use an oracle.

During its computation on input of length n, the machine M cannot produce any string in S of length greater than cn (for some c depending only on M). But the machine can determine the answer to a query about membership of a shorter string in S by simulating an exponential time machine that recognizes S. This shows that L is in DEXT so that S is exponentially low.

7 Characterizations of Complexity Classes

When studying structural complexity theory it is often desirable to have intrinsic characterizations of complexity classes, that is, to describe membership in the class in terms that do not involve the same concepts used in defining the class.

In Sect. 3 intrinsic characterizations of the class **K[log, poly]** and the class of sets with self-producible circuits were described; in both cases the characterizations involved reducibilities.

A different type of characterization by means of reducibilities was introduced by Bennett and Gill [BG81] and refined by Ambos-Spies [Amb86]. Of course, for every set A and every $k \geq 0$, A is in Σ_k^P if and only if for every set B, A is in $\Sigma_k^P(B)$. The characterizations introduced by Bennett and Gill and by Ambos-Spies are different in the sense that they involve reductions to "almost every" oracle set in a measure-theoretic (i.e., probabilistic) sense. Ambos-Spies proved that for every set A, A is in the class P if and only if for almost every set B, A is many-one reducible in polynomial time to B. Bennett and Gill showed that A is in the class BPP if and only if for almost every set B, A is Turing reducible in polynomial time to B. (Recall that BPP is the class defined by probabilistic machines that operate in polynomial time and have bounded error probability.)

Similar characterizations were obtained by Babai and Moran [BM88] and others who were studying the power of interactive proof systems. Generalizing from properties of the class BPP, Schöning [Sch86] defined the "BP-operator" and studied its properties. For any class C, $\mathrm{BP} \cdot \mathrm{C}$ is the class of sets A such that for some B in C, some polynomial $p(n)$, and all $x \in \Sigma^*$,

$$Pr_{p(|x|)}[y : x \in A \text{ if and only if } \langle x, y \rangle \in B(\langle x, y \rangle)] > 3/4,$$

where for any predicate P and natural number m, $Pr_m[y : P(y)]$ is the conditional probability $Pr_m[P/\Sigma^m] = 2^{-m} \times \; \| \; \{y \mid P(y) \text{ and } |y| = m\} \; \|$. As observed by Babai and Moran, the "Arthur-Merlin" class AM can be characterized as $\mathrm{BP} \cdot \mathrm{NP}$, so that it is the nondeterministic counterpart to BPP.

The above results lead to the following question: can membership in $\mathrm{BP} \cdot \Sigma_k^P$ be characterized by means of oracles? That is, is it the case that for every set A, $A \in \mathrm{BP} \cdot \Sigma_k^P$ if and only if for almost every oracle set B, $A \in \Sigma_k^P(B)$?

Tang and Watanabe [TW89] answered this question by showing that for every integer $k \geq 0$ and for every set A, $A \in \mathrm{BP} \cdot \Sigma_k^P$ if and only if for almost every tally set T, $A \in \Sigma_k^P(T)$. The reader should observe that in some sense this is the "minimal" answer. The reason for this informal comment is that it is difficult to see how the results of Tang and Watanabe can hold for any class with "less information" than the class of tally sets, since the class of tally sets is, up to

p-isomorphism, precisely **K[log, poly]**, the class of sets with small generalized Kolmogorov complexity.

The results of Tang and Watanabe were presented at the Second IEEE Conference on Structure in Complexity Theory in June 1988. In October 1988, Nisan and Wigderson [NW88] presented what can be considered as the "maximal" answer to these questions by showing that for every set A, $A \in \text{AM}$ if and only if for almost every set B, $A \in \text{NP}(B)$; this result can be extended to show that for every $k > 0$ and every set A, $A \in \text{BP} \cdot \Sigma_k^P$ if and only if for almost every set B, $A \in \Sigma_k^P(B)$.

Given the characterizations of the classes $BP \cdot \Sigma_k^P$ in the probabilistic polynomial-time hierarchy, it is reasonable to ask if there are similar characterizations of the classes Σ_k^P in the polynomial-time hierarchy. (The reader should note that it is not known whether there exists a k such that $\Sigma_k^P = \text{BP} \cdot \Sigma_k^P$ or whether there exists a k such that $\Sigma_{k+1}^P = \text{BP} \cdot \Sigma_k^P$. However, $\text{BP} \cdot \text{PH} = \text{PH}$ and $\text{BP} \cdot \text{PSPACE} = \text{PSPACE}$.) Tang and Book [TB91] extended the characterization of P given by Ambos-Spies by showing that for every set A, $A \in \text{P}$ if and only if for almost every set B, A is $(\log n)$-Turing reducible in polynomial time to B. (Polynomial-time $(\log n)$-Turing reducibility is simply the restriction of Turing reducibility obtained by demanding that each deterministic polynomial-time bounded oracle machine make at most $c \cdot \log n$ queries in its computation relative to any oracle set on any input of length n, where c is a constant that depends only on the machine.) Thus, no reducibility computed in polynomial time with power strictly between many-one and $(\log n)$-Turing (for example, bounded truth-table lies strictly between these reducibilities) can characterize in this way any class other than P.

Book and Tang [BT90] developed characterizations for each of the classes Σ_k^P (and Π_k^P and Δ_k^P), $k > 0$, by defining the notion of "Σ_k^P-log n-truth-table reducibility, $\leq_{\log n-\text{tt}}^{\Sigma_k^P}$." The characterizations follow easily from the definitions: for every k and for every set A, $A \in \Sigma_k^P$ if and only if for almost every set B, $A \leq_{\log n-\text{tt}}^{\Sigma_k^P} B$. If one uses sets in **K[log, poly]** as the oracle sets, then the analogous results hold so that once again sets in **K[log, poly]** provide "minimal" solutions.

Acknowledgement

It is a pleasure to thank Ms. Shilo Brooks for preparing the manuscript in the style requested by the editor.

References

[All89]   E. Allender. Limitations of the upward separation technique. In *Proc. 16th Int. Colloq. Automata, Languages, and Programming*, Springer-Verlag, Lecture Notes in Computer Science 372:186–194, 1989.

[AH89]   E. Allender and L. Hemachandra. Lower bounds for the low hierarchy. In *Automata, Languages, and Programming*, Springer-Verlag, Lecture Notes in Computer Science 372:31–45, 1989.

[AR88]   E. Allender and R. Rubinstein. P-printable sets. *SIAM J. Computing* 17:1193–1202, 1988.

[AW88]   E. Allender and O. Watanabe. Kolmogorov complexity and degrees of tally sets. *Info. and Computation* 86:160–178, 1990.

[Amb86]   K. Ambos-Spies. Randomness, relativizations, and polynomial reducibilities. In *Proc. 1st Conference on Structure in Complexity Theory*, Springer-Verlag, Lecture Notes in Computer Science 223:23–34, 1986.

[BGS75]   T. Baker, J. Gill, and R. Solovay. Relativizations of the P =? NP question. *SIAM J. Computing* 4:431–442, 1975.

[BB86]   J. Balcázar and R. Book. Sets with small generalized Kolmogorov complexity. *Acta Informatica* 23:679–688, 1986.

[BBS86a]   J. Balcázar, R. Book, and U. Schöning. The polynomial-time hierarchy and sparse oracles. *J. Assoc. Comput. Mach.* 33:603–617, 1986.

[BBS86b]   J. Balcázar, R. Book, and U. Schöning. Sparse sets, lowness, and highness. *SIAM J. Computing* 15:739–747, 1986.

[BDG88]   J. Balcázar, J. Díaz, and J. Gabarró. "Structural Complexity" vol. I and II, Springer-Verlag, 1988 and 1990.

[BM88]   L. Babai and S. Moran. Arthur-Merlin games: a randomized proof system, and a hierarchy of complexity classes. *J. Comput. System Sci.* 36:254–276, 1988.

[BG81]   C. Bennett and J. Gill. Relative to a random oracle, $P^A \neq NP^A \neq co\text{-}NP^A$ with probability one. *SIAM J. Computing* 10:96–113, 1981.

[BH77]   L. Berman and J. Hartmanis. On isomorphism and density of NP and other complete sets. *SIAM J. Computing* 16:305–322, 1977.

[Boo91]   R. Book. Some observations on separating complexity classes. *SIAM J. Computing* 20:246–258, 1991.

[BK88]   R. Book and K. Ko. On sets truth-table reducible to sparse sets. *SIAM J. Computing* 17:903–919, 1988.

[BLS84]   R. Book, T. Long, and A. Selman. Quantitative relativizations of complexity classes. *SIAM J. Computing* 13:461–487, 1984.

[BLW92]   R. Book, J. Lutz, and K. Wagner. On complexity cores and algorithmically random languages. In *Proc. STACS 92*, to appear.

[BORW88]   R. Book, P. Orponen, D. Russo, and O. Watanabe. Lowness properties of sets in the exponential-time hierarchy. *SIAM J. Computing* 17:504–516, 1988.

[BT90]   R. Book and S. Tang. Characterizing polynomial complexity classes by reducibilities. *Mathematical Systems Theory* 23:165–174, 1990.

[GJ79]   M. Garey and D. Johnson. "Computers and Intractability – a guide to the theory of NP-completeness", W. H. Freeman 1979.

[GW91]   R. Gavalda and O. Watanabe. On the computational complexity of small descriptions. In *Proc. 6th IEEE Conference on Structure in Complexity Theory* 89–101, 1991.

[Har83]   J. Hartmanis. Generalized Kolmogorov complexity and the structure of feasible computations. In *24th IEEE Symp. Foundations of Computer Science* 439–445, 1983.

[HH88]   J. Hartmanis and L. Hemachandra. On sparse oracles separating feasible complexity classes. *Info. Processing Letters* 28:291–295, 1988.

[HIS83]   J. Hartmanis, N. Immerman, and V. Sewelson. Sparse sets in NP-P: EXP-TIME versus NEXPTIME. In *Proc. 15th ACM Symp. Theory of Computing* 382–391, 1983.

[Huy87]   D. Huynh. On solving hard problems by polynomial-size circuits. *Info. Processing Letters* 24:171–176, 1987.

[Kan82]   R. Kannan. Circuit-size lower bounds and nonreducibility to sparse sets. *Info. Control* 55:40–56, 1982.

[KL82]   R. Karp and R. Lipton. Turing machines that take advice. *L'Enseignement Mathematique* 28:191–209, 1982.

[Ko85]   K. Ko. Continuous optimization problems and a polynomial hierarchy of real functions. *J. Complexity* 1:210–231, 1985.

[Ko86]   K. Ko. On the notion of infinite pseudorandom sequences: *Theoret. Comput. Sci.* 39:9–33, 1986.

[KS85]   K. Ko and U. Schöning. On circuit-size complexity and the low hierarchy in NP. *SIAM J. Computing* 14:41–51, 1985.

[Kur83]   S. Kurtz. On the random oracle hypothesis. *Info. and Control* 57:40–47, 1983.

[LLS75]   R. Ladner, N. Lynch, and A. Selman. A comparison of polynomial-time reducibilities. *Theoret. Comput. Sci.* 1:103–123, 1975.

[LV90]   M. Li and P. Vitanyi. Applications of Kolmogorov complexity in the theory of computation. *Complexity Theory Retrospective*, A. Selman (ed.), Springer-Verlag Publ. Co. 147–203, 1990.

[Lon82]   T. Long. Strong nondeterministic polynomial-time reducibilities. *Theoret. Comput. Sci.* 21:1–25, 1982.

[Lon85]   T. Long. On restricting the size of oracles compared with restricting access to oracles. *SIAM J. Computing* 14:585–597, 1985.

[LS86]   T. Long and A. Selman. Relativizing complexity classes with sparse oracles. *J. Assoc. Comput. Mach.* 33:616–627, 1986.

[LS91]   T. Long and M.J. Sheu. A refinement of the low and high hierarchies. Submitted for publication, 1991.

[Mar66]   P. Martin-Löf. On the definition of random sequences. *Info. and Control* 9:602–619, 1966.

[NW88]   N. Nisan and A. Wigderson. Hardness vs. randomness. In *Proc. 29th IEEE Symp. Foundations of Comput. Sci.* 2–11, 1988.

[OL91]   M. Ogiwara and A. Lozano. On one query self-reducible sets. In *Proc. 6th IEEE Conference on Structure in Complexity Theory.* 139–151, 1991.

[OW91]   M. Ogiwara and O. Watanabe. On polynomial-time bounded truth-table reducibility of NP sets to sparse sets. *SIAM J. Computing* 20:471–483, 1991.

[Pip79]   N. Pippinger. On simultaneous resource bounds. In *Proc. 20th IEEE Symp. Found. Comput. Sci.* 307–311, 1979.

[Sch83]   U. Schöning. A low and a high hierarchy within NP. *J. Comput. System Sci.* 27:14–28, 1983.

[Sch86]   U. Schöning. Complexity and Structure. In Springer-Verlag, Lecture Notes in Computer Science 211, 1986.

[Sch89]   U. Schöning. Probabilistic complexity classes and lowness. *J. Comput. System Sci.* 39:84–100, 1989.

[Sip83]   M. Sipser. A complexity-theoretic approach to randomness. In *Proc. 15th ACM Symp. Theory of Computing* 330–335, 1983.

[TB88]   S. Tang and R. Book. Separating polynomial-time Turing and truth-table reductions by tally sets. In *Automata, Languages, and Programming*, Springer-Verlag, Lecture Notes in Computer Science 317:591–599, 1988.

[TB91]   S. Tang and R. Book. Polynomial-time reducibilities and "almost-all" oracle sets. *Theoret. Comput. Sci.* 81:36–47, 1991.

[TW89]   S. Tang and O. Watanabe. On tally relativizations of BP-complexity classes. *SIAM J. Computing* 18:449–462, 1989.

[Wat87]   O. Watanabe. A comparison of polynomial time completeness notions. *Theoret. Comput. Sci.* 54:249–265, 1987.

Kolmogorov Complexity, Complexity Cores, and the Distribution of Hardness[*]

David W. Juedes and Jack H. Lutz

Department of Computer Science
Iowa State University
Ames, IA 50011, USA
juedes@iastate.edu, lutz@iastate.edu

Abstract. Problems that are complete for exponential space are provably intractable and known to be exceedingly complex in several technical respects. However, every problem decidable in exponential space is efficiently reducible to every complete problem, so each complete problem must have a highly organized structure. The authors have recently exploited this fact to prove that complete problems are, in two respects, *unusually simple* for problems in expontential space. Specifically, every complete problem must have ususually small complexity cores and unusually low space-bounded Kolmogorov complexity. It follows that the complete problems form a negligibly small subclass of the problems decidable in exponential space. This paper explains the main ideas of this work.

1 Introduction

It is well understood that an object that is complex in one sense may be simple in another. In this paper we show that every decision problem that is complex in one standard, complexity-theoretic sense *must be* unusually simple in two other such senses.

Throughout this paper, the terms "problem," "decision problem," and "language" are synonyms and refer to a set $A \subseteq \{0,1\}^*$, i.e., a set of binary strings. The three notions of complexity considered are completeness (or hardness) for a complexity class, space-bounded Kolmogorov complexity, and the existence of large complexity cores. (All terms are defined and discussed in §§2-6 below, so this paper is essentially self-contained.) In a certain setting, we prove that every problem that is complete for a complexity class must have unusually low space-bounded Kolmogorov complexity and unusually small complexity cores. Thus complexity in one sense *implies* simplicity in another.

To be specific, we work with the complexity class ESPACE = DSPACE(2^{linear}). There are two related reasons for this choice. First, ESPACE

---

[*] This research was supported in part by National Science Foundation Grants CCR-8809238 and CCR-9157382 and in part by DIMACS, where the second author was a visitor while part of this work was carried out.

has a rich, well-behaved structure that is well enough understood that we can prove absolute results, unblemished by oracles or unproven hypotheses. In particular, much is known about the distribution of Kolmogorov complexities in ESPACE [Lut92a, §4 below], while very little is known at lower complexity levels. Second, the structure of ESPACE is closely related to the structure of polynomial complexity classes. For example, Hartmanis and Yesha [HY84] have shown that

$$\text{E} \subsetneq \text{ESPACE} \iff \text{P} \subsetneq \text{P/Poly} \cap \text{PSPACE}.$$

This, together with the first reason, suggests that the separation of P from PSPACE might best be achieved by separating E from ESPACE. We thus seek a detailed, quantitative account of the structure of ESPACE.

For simplicity of exposition, we work with polynomial time, many-one reducibility ("$\leq_m^P$-reducibility"), introduced by Karp[Kar72]. Problems that are $\leq_m^P$-complete for ESPACE have been exhibited by Meyer and Stockmeyer [MS72], Stockmeyer and Chandra[SC89], and others. Such problems are correctly regarded as exceedingly complex. They are provably intractable in terms of computational time and space. They have exponential circuit-size complexity [Kan82], weakly exponential space-bounded Kolmogorov complexity [Huy86], and dense complexity cores [OS86, Huy87]. Problems that are $\leq_m^P$-hard for ESPACE have all these properties and need not even be recursive.

Notwithstanding these lower bounds on the complexity of $\leq_m^P$-hard problems for ESPACE, we will prove in §6 below that such problems are *unusually simple* in two respects. The word "unusually" here requires some explanation.

Suppose that we choose a language $A \subseteq \{0,1\}^*$ probabilistically, according to a random experiment in which an independent toss of a fair coin is used to decide membership of each string $x \in \{0,1\}^*$ in A. For a set X of languages, let $\Pr(X) = \Pr_A[A \in X]$ denote the probability that $A \in X$ (" the probability that event X occurs") in this experiment, provided that this probability exists. (All sets X of languages considered in this paper are Lebesgue measurable, so that $\Pr(X)$ is well-defined. Thus we will not concern ourselves with issues of measurability.) If the event X has the property that $\Pr(X) = 1$, then we say that *almost every* language $A \subseteq \{0,1\}^*$ is in X. In such a case, the complement X^c of X has probability $\Pr(X^c) = 0$, so it is *unusual* for a language A to be in X^c. In particular, a language A is *unusually simple* in the sense of a given complexity measure if there is a lower complexity bound that holds for almost all languages but does not hold for A.

This probabilistic notion of "almost every" and "unusual" is intuitive and suggestive of our intent, but is not strong enough for our purposes. As we have noted, we seek to understand the structure of ESPACE. Accordingly, we will prove in §6 below that $\leq_m^P$-hard problems for ESPACE are *unusually simple for problems in* ESPACE in two specific senses. This means that, in each of these senses, there is a lower complexity bound that holds for almost every language in ESPACE but does not hold for languages that are $\leq_m^P$-hard for ESPACE. This immediately yields a quantitative result on the distribution of $\leq_m^P$-complete problems in ESPACE: Almost every language in ESPACE fails to be $\leq_m^P$-complete.

But what does it mean for "almost every language in ESPACE" to have some property? Naively, we would like to say that almost every language is ESPACE is in some set X if, in the above random experiment, $\Pr(X|\text{ESPACE})$ $= \Pr_A[A \in X | A \in \text{ESPACE}] = 1$. The problem here is that ESPACE is a countable set of languages, so $\Pr_A[A \in \text{ESPACE}] = 0$, so the conditional probability $\Pr(X|\text{ESPACE})$ is not defined. We thus turn to *resource-bounded measure*, a complexity-theoretic generalization of Lebesgue measure developed by Lutz[Lut92a, Lut92b]. Suppose we are given a *resource bound*, e.g., the set pspace, consisting of all functions computable in polynomial space. Then resource-bounded measure theory defines the pspace-*measure* $\mu_{\text{pspace}}(X)$ of a set X of languages (provided that X is pspace-measurable). In all cases, $0 \leq \mu_{\text{pspace}}(X) \leq 1$. If $\mu_{\text{pspace}}(X) = 0$ or $\mu_{\text{pspace}}(X) = 1$, then $\Pr(X) = 0$ or $\Pr(X) = 1$, respectively, but the pspace-measure conditions are much stronger than this: It is shown in [Lut92a, Lut92b] that, if $\mu_{\text{pspace}}(X) = 0$, then $X \cap \text{ESPACE}$ is a *negligibly small* subset of ESPACE. In fact, pspace-measure induces a natural, internal, measure structure on ESPACE. In this structure, a set X of languages has *measure 0 in* ESPACE, and we write $\mu(X|\text{ESPACE}) = 0$, if $\mu_{\text{pspace}}(X \cap \text{ESPACE}) = 0$. A set X has *measure 1 in* ESPACE, and we write $\mu(X|\text{ESPACE}) = 1$, if $\mu(X^c|\text{ESPACE}) = 0$. Finally, we say that *almost every* language in ESPACE is in some set X of languages if $\mu(X|\text{ESPACE}) = 1$. In §3 below we summarize those aspects of resource-bounded measure that are used in this paper.

Kolmogorov complexity, discussed in several papers in this volume, was introduced by Solomonoff[Sol64], Kolmogorov[Kol65], and Chaitin[Cha66]. Resource-bounded Kolmogorov complexity has been investigated extensively [Kol65, Har83, Sip83, Lev84, Lon86, BB86, Huy86, Ko86, AR88, All89, AW90, Lut90, Lut92a, etc.]. In this paper we work with the *space-bounded Kolmogorov complexity* of languages. Roughly speaking, for $A \subseteq \{0,1\}^*$, $n \in \mathbf{N}$, and a space bound t, the space-bounded Kolmogorov complexity $KS^t(A_{=n})$ is the length of the shortest program that prints the 2^n-bit characteristic string of $A_{=n} = A \cap \{0,1\}^n$, using at most t units of workspace. This quantity $KS^t(A_{=n})$ is frequently interpreted as the "amount of information" that is contained in $A_{=n}$ and is "accessible" by computation using $\leq t$ space. In §4 below, we review the precise formulation of this definition (and the analoguous definition of $KS^t(A_{\leq n})$) and some of its properties. After surveying some recent complexity-theoretic applications of an almost-everywhere lower bound on $KS^t(A_{\leq n})$[Lut92a], we prove a new almost everywhere lower bound result (Theorem 6/Corollary 7) showing that for all $c \in \mathbf{N}$ and $\epsilon > 0$, almost every language $A \in \text{ESPACE}$ has space-bounded Kolmogorov complexity

$$KS^{2^{cn}}(A_{=n}) > 2^n - n^\epsilon \text{ a.e.}$$

(This improves the $2^n - 2^{\epsilon n}$ lower bound of [Lut92a].) It should be noted that the proof of this result is the only direct use of resource-bounded measure in this paper. All the measure-theoretic results in §5-6 are proven by appeal to this almost everywhere lower bound on space-bounded Kolmogorov complexity.

In §5 , we review the fundamental notion of a *complexity core*, introduced by Lynch[Lyn75] and investigated by many others [Du85, ESY85, Orp86, OS86,

BD87, Huy87, RO87, BDR88, DB89, Ye90, etc.]. Intuitively, a complexity core for a language A is a fixed set K of inputs such that *every* machine whose decisions are consistent with A fails to decide efficiently on almost all elements of K. The meanings of "efficiently" and "almost all" are parameters of this definition that may be varied according to the context. In §5, in order to better understand ESPACE, we work with $\mathrm{DSPACE}(2^{cn})$-complexity cores (for fixed constants c). In Theorem 9 we prove that any upper bound on the densities of $\mathrm{DSPACE}(2^{cn})$-complexity cores for a language A implies a corresponding upper bound on the space-bounded Kolmogorov complexity of A. The quantitative details imply that almost every language in ESPACE has co-sparse complexity cores.

In §6, we apply these results to our main topic, which is the complexity and distribution of $\leq_m^P$-hard problems for ESPACE. It is well-known that such problems are not feasibly decidable and must obey certain lower bounds on their complexities. As noted above, Huynh[Huy86] has proven that every $\leq_m^P$-hard for ESPACE has weakly exponential (i.e., $> 2^{n^\epsilon}$ for some $\epsilon > 0$) space-bounded Kolmogorov complexity; and Orponen and Schöning[OS86] have (essentially) proven that every $\leq_m^P$-hard language for ESPACE has a dense $\mathrm{DSPACE}(2^{cn})$-complexity core. Intuitively, such results are not surprising, as we do not expect hard problems to be simple. However, in §6, we prove that these hard problems *must* be simple in that they obey *upper* bounds on their complexities. In Theorem 13 we prove that every $\mathrm{DSPACE}(2^n)$-complexity core of every $\leq_m^P$-hard language for ESPACE must have a dense complement. Note that this upper bound is the "mirror image" of the Orponen-Schöning lower bound cited above: Every hard problem has a dense core, but this core's complement must also be dense. In Theorem 14 we use Theorems 9 and 13 to prove that every $\leq_m^P$-hard language for ESPACE has space-bounded Kolmogorov complexity that is less than 2^n by a weakly exponential amount. Again, note that this upper bound is the "mirror image" of the Huynh lower bound cited above.

We have seen that almost every language in ESPACE has co-sparse complexity cores and essentially maximal Kolmogorov complexity. Thus our upper bounds imply that the $\leq_m^P$-complete problems have *unusually low* space-bounded Kolmogorov complexity and *unusually small* complexity cores for problems in ESPACE. It follows that the $\leq_m^P$-complete problems form a measure 0 subset of ESPACE.

In order to simplify the exposition of the main ideas and to highlight the role played by Kolmogorov complexity, we do not state our results in the strongest possible form in this volume. The interested reader may wish to consult the technical paper [JL92] for a more thorough treatment of these issues. For example, it is shown in [JL92] that $\leq_m^P$-hard problems for E have unusually small complexity cores, whence the $\leq_m^P$-complete problems for E form a measure 0 subset of E. (Note added in proof: Recently, Mayordomo[May91] has independently proven that the $\leq_m^P$-complete problems for E form a measure 0 subset of E. Mayordomo's proof exploits the Berman [Ber76] result that every $\leq_m^P$-complete problem for E has an infinite subset in P.)

2 Preliminaries

Most of our notation and terminology is standard. We deal with *strings, languages, functions*, and *classes*. Strings are finite sequences of characters over the alphabet $\{0,1\}$; we write $\{0,1\}^*$ for the set of all strings. Languages are sets of strings. Functions usually map $\{0,1\}^*$ into $\{0,1\}^*$. A class is either a set of languages or a set of functions.

When a property $\phi(n)$ of the natural numbers is true for all but finitely many $n \in \mathbf{N}$, we say that $\phi(n)$ holds *almost everywhere (a.e.)* . Similarly, $\phi(n)$ holds *infinitely often (i.o.)*, if $\phi(n)$ is true for infinitely many $n \in \mathbf{N}$. We write $[\![\phi]\!]$ for the Boolean value of a condition ϕ. That is, $[\![\phi]\!] = 1$ if ϕ is true, 0 if ϕ is false.

If $x \in \{0,1\}^*$ is a string, we write $|x|$ for the *length* of x. If $A \subseteq \{0,1\}^*$ is a language, then we write A^c, $A_{\leq n}$, and $A_{=n}$ for $\{0,1\}^* \setminus A$, $A \cap \{0,1\}^{\leq n}$, and $A \cap \{0,1\}^n$ respectively. The sequence of strings over $\{0,1\}$, $s_0 = \lambda, s_1 = 0, s_2 = 1, s_3 = 00, ...$, is referred to as the standard lexicographic enumeration of $\{0,1\}^*$. The *characteristic string* of $A_{\leq n}$ is the N-bit string

$$\chi_{A_{\leq n}} = [\![s_0 \in A]\!][\![s_1 \in A]\!]...[\![s_{N-1} \in A]\!],$$

where $N = |\{0,1\}^{\leq n}| = 2^{n+1} - 1$.

We use the string pairing function $\langle x, y \rangle = bd(x)01y$, where $bd(x)$ is x with each bit doubled (e.g., $bd(1101) = 11110011$). Note that $|\langle x, y \rangle| = 2|x| + |y| + 2$ for all $x, y \in \{0,1\}^*$. For each $g : \{0,1\}^* \to \{0,1\}^*$ and $k \in \mathbf{N}$, we also define the function $g_k : \{0,1\}^* \to \{0,1\}^*$ by $g_k(x) = g(\langle 0^k, x \rangle)$ for all $x \in \{0,1\}^*$.

If A is a finite set, we denote its cardinality by $|A|$. A language D is *dense* if there exists some constant $\epsilon > 0$ such that $|D_{\leq n}| > 2^{n^\epsilon}$ a.e. A language S is *sparse* if there exists a polynomial p such that $|S_{\leq n}| \leq p(n)$ a.e.. A language S is *co-sparse* if S^c is sparse.

All *machines* here are deterministic Turing machines. A machine M is an *acceptor* if M on input x either accepts, rejects or does not halt. The language accepted by a machine M is denoted by $L(M)$. A machine M is a *transducer* defining the function f_M if M on input x outputs $f_M(x)$. The functions $time_M(x)$ and $space_M(x)$ represent the number of steps and tape cells, respectively, that the machine M uses on input x. Some of our machines take inputs of the form (x, n), where $x \in \{0,1\}^*$ and $n \in \mathbf{N}$. These machines are assumed to have two input tapes, one for x and the other for the standard binary representation $\beta(n) \in \{0,1\}^*$ of n.

The following standard time- and space-bounded uniform complexity classes are used in this paper.

$$\mathrm{DTIME}(t(n)) = \{L(M) \mid (\exists c)(\forall x) time_M(x) \leq c \cdot t(|x|) + c\}$$
$$\mathrm{DTIMEF}(t(n)) = \{f_M \mid (\exists c)(\forall x) time_M(x) \leq c \cdot t(|x|) + c\}$$
$$\mathrm{DSPACE}(s(n)) = \{L(M) \mid (\exists c)(\forall x) space_M(x) \leq c \cdot s(|x|) + c\}$$
$$\mathrm{DSPACEF}(s(n)) = \{f_M \mid (\exists c)(\forall x) space_M(x) \leq c \cdot s(|x|) + c\}$$
$$\mathrm{P} = \bigcup_{i=1}^{\infty} \mathrm{DTIME}(n^i),$$

$$\text{PSPACE} = \bigcup_{i=1}^{\infty} \text{DSPACE}(n^i),$$

$$\text{PF} = \bigcup_{i=1}^{\infty} \text{DTIMEF}(n^i),$$

$$\text{E} = \bigcup_{c=1}^{\infty} \text{DTIME}(2^{cn}), \text{ and}$$

$$\text{ESPACE} = \bigcup_{c=1}^{\infty} \text{DSPACE}(2^{cn}).$$

The nonuniform complexity class P/Poly, mentioned in §1, is defined in terms of machines with advice. An *advice function* is a function $h : \mathbf{N} \to \{0,1\}^*$. A language A is in P/Poly if and only if there exist $B \in \text{P}$, a polynomial p, and an advice function h such that $|h(k)| \le p(k)$ and $x \in A \iff \langle x, h(|x|)\rangle \in B$ for all $k \in \mathbf{N}$ and $x \in \{0,1\}^*$. It is well-known [KL80] that P/Poly consists exactly of those languages that are computed by polynomial-size Boolean circuits.

If A and B are languages, then a *polynomial time, many-one reduction* (briefly $\le_m^P$-*reduction*) of A to B is a function $f \in \text{PF}$ such that $A = f^{-1}(B) = \{x \mid f(x) \in B\}$. A $\le_m^P$-*reduction of A* is a function $f \in \text{PF}$ that is a $\le_m^P$-reduction of A to some language B. Note that f is a $\le_m^P$-reduction of A if and only if f is $\le_m^P$-reduction of A to $f(A) = \{f(x) \mid x \in A\}$. We say that A is *polynomial time, many-one reducible* (briefly, $\le_m^P$-*reducible*) to B, and we write $A \le_m^P B$, if there exists a $\le_m^P$-reduction f of A to B. In this case, we also say that $A \le_m^P B$ *via* f.

A language H is $\le_m^P$-*hard* for a class $\mathcal{C}$ of languages if $A \le_m^P H$ for all $A \in \mathcal{C}$. A language C is $\le_m^P$-*complete* for $\mathcal{C}$ if $C \in \mathcal{C}$ and C is $\le_m^P$-hard for $\mathcal{C}$. If $\mathcal{C} = \text{NP}$, this is the usual notion of NP-completeness[GJ79]. In this paper we are especially concerned with languages that are $\le_m^P$-hard or $\le_m^P$-complete for ESPACE.

3 Resource-Bounded Measure

In this section we very briefly give some fundamentals of resource-bounded measure, where the resource bound is polynomial space. (This is the resource bound that endows ESPACE with measure structure.) For more details, examples, motivation, and proofs, see [Lut92a, Lut92b].

The *characteristic sequence* of a language $A \subseteq \{0,1\}^*$ is the binary sequence $\chi_A \in \{0,1\}^\infty$ defined by $\chi_A[i] = [\![s_i \in A]\!]$ for all $i \in \mathbf{N}$. (Recall from §2, that $s_0, s_i, s_2, \ldots$ is the standard enumeration of $\{0,1\}^*$.) For $x \in \{0,1\}^*$ and $A \subseteq \{0,1\}^*$, we say that x is a *prefix*, or *partial specification*, of A if x is a prefix of χ_A, i.e., if there exists $y \in \{0,1\}^\infty$ such that $\chi_A = xy$. In this case, we write $x \sqsubseteq A$. The *cylinder specified by* a string $x \in \{0,1\}^*$ is

$$C_x = \{A \subseteq \{0,1\}^* \mid x \sqsubseteq A\}.$$

We let $\mathbf{D} = \{m2^{-n} \mid m, n \in \mathbf{N}\}$ be the set of *nonnegative dyadic rationals*. Many functions in this paper take their values in $\mathbf{D}$ or in $[0, \infty)$, the set of nonnegative real numbers. In fact, with the exception of some functions that map into $[0, \infty)$, all our functions are of the form $f : X \to Y$, where each of the sets X, Y is $\mathbf{N}$, $\{0,1\}^*$, $\mathbf{D}$, or some cartesian product of these sets. Formally, in order to have uniform criteria for their computational complexity, we regard all such functions as mapping $\{0,1\}^*$ into $\{0,1\}^*$. For example, a function $f : \mathbf{N}^2 \times \{0,1\}^* \to \mathbf{N} \times \mathbf{D}$ is formally interpreted as a function $\tilde{f} : \{0,1\}^* \to \{0,1\}^*$. Under this interpretation, $f(i, j, w) = (k, q)$ means that $\tilde{f}(\langle 0^i, \langle 0^j, w \rangle \rangle) = \langle 0^k, \langle u, v \rangle \rangle$, where u and v are the binary representations of the integer and fractional parts of q, respectively. Moreover, we only care about the values of $\tilde{f}$ for arguments of the form $\langle 0^i, \langle 0^j, w \rangle \rangle$, and we insist that these values have the form $\langle 0^k, \langle u, v \rangle \rangle$ for such arguments.

For a function $f : \mathbf{N} \times X \to Y$ and $k \in \mathbf{N}$, we define the function $f_k : X \to Y$ by $f_k(x) = f(k, x) = f(\langle 0^k, x \rangle)$. We then regard f as a "uniform enumeration" of the functions $f_0, f_1, f_2, \dots$. For a function $f : \mathbf{N}^n \times X \to Y$ ($n \geq 2$), we write $f_{k,l} = (f_k)_l$, etc.

We work with the resource bound

$$\text{pspace} = \{f : \{0,1\}^* \to \{0,1\}^* \mid f \text{ is computable in polynomial space}\}.$$

(The length $|f(x)|$ of the output *is* included as part of the space used in computing f.)

Resource-bounded measure was originally developed in terms of "modulated covering by cylinders" [Lut90]. Though the main results of this paper are true, the underlying development was technically flawed. This situation is remedied in [Lut92a, Lut92b], where resource-bounded measure is reformulated in terms of density functions. We review relevant aspects of the latter formulation here.

A *density function* is a function $d : \{0,1\}^* \to [0, \infty)$ satisfying

$$d(x) \geq \frac{d(x0) + d(x1)}{2}$$

for all $x \in \{0,1\}^*$. The *global value* of a density function d is $d(\lambda)$. An n-dimensional *density system (n-DS)* is a function $d : \mathbf{N}^n \times \{0,1\}^* \to [0, \infty)$ such that $d_{\mathbf{k}}$ is a density function for every $\mathbf{k} \in \mathbf{N}^n$. It is sometimes convenient to regard a density function as a 0-DS.

A *computation* of an n-DS d is a function $\hat{d} : \mathbf{N}^{n+1} \times \{0,1\}^* \to \mathbf{D}$ such that

$$\left| \hat{d}_{\mathbf{k},r}(x) - d_{\mathbf{k}}(x) \right| \leq 2^{-r} \tag{1}$$

for all $\mathbf{k} \in \mathbf{N}^n$, $r \in \mathbf{N}$, and $x \in \{0,1\}^*$. A pspace-*computation* of an n-DS d is a computation $\hat{d}$ such that $\hat{d} \in$ pspace. An n-DS is pspace-*computable* if there exists a pspace-computation $\hat{d}$ of d.

The *set covered by* a density function d is

$$S[d] = \bigcup_{d(x) \geq 1} C_x.$$

A density function d *covers* a set X of languages if $X \subseteq S[d]$. A *null cover* of a set X of languages is a 1-DS d such that, for all $k \in \mathbf{N}$, d_k covers X with global value $d_k(\lambda) \leq 2^{-k}$. It is easy to show [Lut92b] that a set X of languages has classical Lebesgue measure 0 (*i.e.*, probability 0 in the coin-tossing random experiment) if and only if there exists a null cover of X. In this paper we are interested in the situation where the null cover d is pspace-computable.

Definition 1. Let X be a set of languages and let X^c denote the complement of X.

(1) A pspace-*null cover* of X is a null cover of X that is pspace-computable.
(2) X has pspace-*measure 0*, and we write $\mu_{\text{pspace}}(X) = 0$, if there exists a pspace-null cover of X.
(3) X has pspace-*measure 1*, and we write $\mu_{\text{pspace}}(X) = 1$, if $\mu_{\text{pspace}}(X^c) = 0$.
(4) X has *measure 0 in* ESPACE, and we write $\mu(X \mid \text{ESPACE}) = 0$, if $\mu_{\text{pspace}}(X \cap \text{ESPACE}) = 0$.
(5) X has *measure 1 in* ESPACE, and we write $\mu(X \mid \text{ESPACE}) = 1$, if $\mu(X^c \mid \text{ESPACE}) = 0$. In this case, we say that X contains *almost every* language in ESPACE.

It is shown in [Lut92a, Lut92b] that these definitions endow ESPACE with internal measure-theoretic structure. Specifically, if $\mathcal{I}$ is either the collection $\mathcal{I}_{\text{pspace}}$ of all pspace-measure 0 sets or the collection $\mathcal{I}_{\text{ESPACE}}$ of all sets of measure 0 in ESPACE, then $\mathcal{I}$ is a "pspace-ideal," *i.e.*, is closed under subsets, finite unions, and "pspace-unions" (countable unions that can be generated in polynomial space). More importantly, it is shown that the ideal $\mathcal{I}_{\text{ESPACE}}$ is a *proper* ideal, *i.e.*, that ESPACE does *not* have measure 0 in ESPACE.

Our proof of Theorem 6 below does not proceed directly from the above definitions. Instead we use a sufficient condition, proved in [Lut92a], for a set to have pspace-measure 0. To state this condition we need a polynomial notion of convergence for infinite series. All our series here consist of nonnegative terms. A *modulus* for a series $\sum\limits_{n=0}^{\infty} a_n$ is a function $m : \mathbf{N} \to \mathbf{N}$ such that

$$\sum_{n=m(j)}^{\infty} a_n \leq 2^{-j}$$

for all $j \in \mathbf{N}$. A series is p-*convergent* if it has a modulus that is a polynomial.

The following sufficient condition for a set to have pspace-measure 0 is a special case (for pspace) of a resource-bounded generalization of the classical first Borel-Cantelli lemma.

Lemma 2. *(Lutz[Lut92a]). If d is a pspace-computable 1-DS such that the series* $\sum\limits_{n=0}^{\infty} d_n(\lambda)$ *is p-convergent, then*

$$\mu_{\text{pspace}}\left(\bigcap_{t=0}^{\infty} \bigcup_{n=t}^{\infty} S[d_n]\right) = \mu_{\text{pspace}}(\{A \mid A \in S[d_n] \ i.o.\}) = 0.$$

4 Space-Bounded Kolmogorov Complexity

In this section we present the basic facts about space-bounded Kolmogorov complexity that are used in this paper.

Some terminology and notation will be useful. For a fixed machine M and "program" $\pi \in \{0,1\}^*$ for M, we say that "$M(\pi, n) = w$ in $\leq s$ space" if M, on input (π, n), outputs the string $w \in \{0,1\}^*$ and halts without using more than s cells of workspace. We are especially interested in situations where the output is of the form $\chi_{A=n}$ or of the form $\chi_{A\leq n}$, i.e., the 2^n-bit characteristic string of $A_{=n}$ or the $(2^{n+1} - 1)$-bit characteristic string of $A_{\leq n}$, for some language A.

Given a machine M, a space bound $s : \mathbf{N} \to \mathbf{N}$, a language $A \subseteq \{0,1\}^*$, and a natural number n, the $s(n)$-*space-bounded Kolmogorov complexity* of $A_{=n}$ relative to M is

$$KS_M^{s(n)}(A_{=n}) = min\{|\pi|\,\big|\,M(\pi, n) = \chi_{A_{=n}} \text{ in } \leq s(n) \text{ space } \}.$$

Similarly, the $s(n)$-*space-bounded Kolmogorov complexity* of $A_{\leq n}$ relative to M is

$$KS_M^{s(n)}(A_{\leq n}) = min\{|\pi|\,\big|\,M(\pi, n) = \chi_{A_{\leq n}} \text{ in } \leq s(n) \text{ space } \}.$$

Well-known simulation techniques show that there is a machine U that is *optimal* in the sense that for each machine M there is a constant c such that for all s, A and n, we have

$$KS_U^{c \cdot s(n)+c}(A_{=n}) \leq KS_M^{s(n)}(A_{=n}) + c$$

and

$$KS_U^{c \cdot s(n)+c}(A_{\leq n}) \leq KS_M^{s(n)}(A_{\leq n}) + c.$$

As is standard in this subject, we fix an optimal machine U and omit it from the notation.

We now recall the following almost-everywhere lower bound result.

Theorem 3. *(Lutz[Lut92a]). Let $c \in \mathbf{N}$ and $\epsilon > 0$.*

(a) If

$$X = \{A \subseteq \{0,1\}^* | KS^{2^{cn}}(A_{=n}) > 2^n - 2^{\epsilon n} \text{ a.e.}\},$$

then $\mu_{\text{pspace}}(X) = \mu(X|\text{ESPACE}) = 1$.

(b) If

$$Y = \{A \subseteq \{0,1\}^* | KS^{2^{cn}}(A_{\leq n}) > 2^{n+1} - 2^{\epsilon n} \text{ a.e.}\},$$

then $\mu_{\text{pspace}}(Y) = \mu(Y|\text{ESPACE}) = 1$.

Informally, Theorem 3 says that $KS(A_{=n})$ and $KS(A_{\leq n})$ are very high for almost all n, for all almost all $A \in \text{ESPACE}$. This lower bound has been useful in a variety of applications in complexity theory, especially in contexts involving Boolean circuits.

Example 1. The *circuit-size complexity* of a language $A \subseteq \{0,1\}^*$ is the function $CS_A : \mathbf{N} \to \mathbf{N}$ defined as follows: For each $n \in \mathbf{N}$, $CS_A(n)$ is the minimum size (number of gates) required for an n-input, 1-output Boolean (acyclic, combinational) circuit to decide the set $A_{=n}$. (See [Lut92a, BDG88, Weg87] for details of the circuit model, which can be varied in minor ways without affecting this discussion.) Circuit-size complexity has been investigated extensively for over forty years. Shannon[Sha49] proved that *almost every* language $A \subseteq \{0,1\}^*$ has circuit-size complexity

$$CS_A(n) > \frac{2^n}{n} \text{ a.e.} \tag{4.1}$$

That is, if we choose the language $A \subseteq \{0,1\}^*$ probabilistically, according to a random experiment in which an independent toss of a fair coin is used to decide membership of each string $x \in \{0,1\}^*$ in A, then

$$\mathrm{Pr}_A[CS_A(n) > \frac{2^n}{n} \text{ a.e.}] = 1. \tag{4.2}$$

Lupanov[Lup58] proved that *every* language $A \subseteq \{0,1\}^*$ has circuit-size complexity

$$CS_A(n) < \frac{2^n}{n}(1 + O(\frac{1}{\sqrt{n}})). \tag{4.3}$$

Since the lower bound (4.1) and the upper bound (4.3) have asympotic ratio 1, these results say that *almost every* language A has essentially maximum circuit-size complexity almost everywhere. Lupanov named this phenomenon the *Shannon effect.*

Lutz[Lut92a] used Theorem 3 to investigate the Shannon effect in ESPACE. The upper bound (4.3) applies *a fortiori* to languages in ESPACE, but the lower bound (4.2) does not directly say anything about ESPACE because $\mathrm{Pr}_A[A \notin \mathrm{ESPACE}] = 1$ in the same random experiment. However, it is not difficult to see that an upper bound on $CS_A(n)$ *implies* an upper bound on $KS(A_{=n})$. In fact, Lutz[Lut92a] showed that the quantitave details of this relation, combined with Theorem 3(a), imply that, for every real $\alpha < 1$, almost every language $A \in \mathrm{ESPACE}$ (and, as a corollary, almost every language $A \subseteq \{0,1\}^*$) has circuit-size complexity

$$CS_A(n) > \frac{2^n}{n}(1 + \frac{\alpha \log n}{n}) \text{ a.e.}$$

Thus the Shannon effect holds with full force in ESPACE.

Example 2. Nisan and Wigderson[NW88] proved that, if E contains a language A that is, in a certain technical sense, "very hard to approximate with circuits," then this language A can be used to construct a pseudorandom generator that is fast enough and secure enough to establish the condition P = BPP. Subsequent to this, Lutz[Lut91] proved that there is a constant $c \in \mathbf{N}$ such that every language A that is *not* "very hard to approximate with circuits" has space-bounded Kolmogorov complexity

$$KS^{2^{cn}}(A_{=n}) < 2^n - 2^{\frac{n}{4}} \text{ i.o.}$$

By Theorem 3(a), this implies that almost every language $A \in$ ESPACE is "very hard to approximate with circuits." This fact, together with the result of Nisan and Wigderson, immediately yields an *upward measure separation* theorem, stating that

$$\mathrm{P} \neq \mathrm{BPP} \Rightarrow \mu(\mathrm{E}|\mathrm{ESPACE}) = 0.$$

(Hartmanis and Yesha[HY84] had previously shown that $\mathrm{P} \neq \mathrm{BPP} \Rightarrow \mathrm{E} \subsetneq$ ESPACE.)

In each of the above examples, space-bounded Kolmogorov complexity is used to prove that some set Z of languages has measure 1 in ESPACE. In each case, the method is simply to prove that every language *not* in Z has *unusually low* space-bounded Kolmogorov complexity for languages in ESPACE. That is, every language not in Z has space-bounded Kolmogorov complexity that infinitely often violates the lower bounds obeyed by almost every element of ESPACE.

In this paper we will use similar arguments to show that almost every language $A \in$ ESPACE fails to be $\leq_m^P$-complete for ESPACE. In fact, we will prove that every language H that is $\leq_m^P$-hard for ESPACE has *unusually low* space-bounded Kolmogorov complexity, by which we mean space-bounded Kolmogorov complexity that violates a lower bound obeyed by almost every language $A \in$ ESPACE (and almost every language $A \subseteq \{0,1\}^*$).

As it turns out, Theorem 3 is not strong enough for this purpose! We will show that every $\leq_m^P$-hard language H for ESPACE has an unusually low upper bound on its space bounded Kolmogorov complexity, but this upper bound will *not* violate the lower bounds of Theorem 3. We are thus led to ask how tight the lower bounds of Theorem 3 are.

We first consider Theorem 3(b). Martin-Löf [Mar71] has shown that, for every real $a > 1$, almost every language $A \subseteq \{0,1\}^*$ has space-bounded Kolmogorov complexity

$$KS^{2^{cn}}(A_{\leq n}) > 2^{n+1} - an \quad \text{a.e.} \tag{4.4}$$

(In fact, Martin-Löf showed that this holds even in the absence of a space bound.) The following known bounds show that the lower bound (4.4) is tight.

Theorem 4. *There exist constants $c_1, c_2 \in \mathbf{N}$ such that every language A satisfies the following two conditions.*

(i) $KS^{2^n}(A_{\leq n}) < 2^{n+1} + c_1$ *for all n.*
(ii) $KS^{2^{c_2 n}}(A_{\leq n}) < 2^{n+1} - n$ *i.o.*

(Part (i) of Theorem 4 is well known and obvious. Part (ii), proven in [Lut92a], extends a result of Martin-Löf [Mar71].)

Since the bound of Theorem 3(b) is considerably lower than that of (4.4), one might expect to improve Theorem 3(b). However, the following upper bound shows that Theorem 3(b) is also tight. (In comparing Theorems 3(b) and 5 it is critical to note the order in which A and ϵ are quantified.)

Theorem 5. *For every language $A \in$ ESPACE, there exists a real $\epsilon > 0$ such that*

$$KS^{2^{2^n}}(A_{\leq n}) < 2^{n+1} - 2^{\epsilon n} \quad a.e.$$

Proof. Fix $A \in$ ESPACE and $a \in \mathbf{N}$ such that $A \in$ DSPACE(2^{an}). For each $n \in \mathbf{N}$, let $n' = \lfloor \frac{n}{a+1} \rfloor$ and let y_n be the string of length $2^{n+1} - 2^{n'+1}$ such that $\chi_{A_{\leq n}} = \chi_{A_{\leq n'}} y_n$. Let M be a machine that, on input (y, n), computes $\chi_{A_{\leq n'}}$ using $\leq 2^{an'}$ space and then outputs $\chi_{A_{\leq n'}} y$. Let c be the optimality constant for the machine M (given by the definition of the optimal machine U at the beginning of this section). Then $M(y_n, n)$ outputs $\chi_{A_{\leq n}}$ in $\leq 2^{an'}$ space, so for all sufficiently large n, we have

$$\begin{aligned}
KS^{2^{2^n}}(A_{\leq n}) &\leq KS_M^{2^{an'}}(A_{\leq n}) + c \\
&\leq |y_n| + c \\
&= 2^{n+1} - 2^{n'+1} + c \\
&< 2^{n+1} - 2^{\epsilon n},
\end{aligned}$$

where $\epsilon = \frac{1}{a+2}$.

Thus we cannot hope to improve Theorem 3(b).

An elementary counting argument shows that, for every $c \in \mathbf{N}$, there *exists* a language $A \in$ ESPACE with $KS^{2^{cn}}(A_{=n}) \geq 2^n$ for all $n \in \mathbf{N}$. This suggests that the prospect for improving Theorem 3(a) may be more hopeful. In fact, we have the following almost-everywhere lower bound result.

Theorem 6. *Let $c \in \mathbf{N}$ and let $f : \mathbf{N} \to \mathbf{N}$ be such that $f \in$ pspace and $\sum_{n=0}^{\infty} 2^{-f(n)}$ is p-convergent. If*

$$X = \{ A \subseteq \{0,1\}^* \mid KS^{2^{cn}}(A_{=n}) > 2^n - f(n) \ a.e. \},$$

then $\mu_{\mathrm{pspace}}(X) = \mu(X \mid$ ESPACE$) = 1$.

Proof. Assume the hypothesis. By Lemma 2, it suffices to exhibit a pspace-computable 1-DS d such that

$$\sum_{n=0}^{\infty} d_n(\lambda) \text{ is p-convergent} \tag{4.5}$$

and

$$X^c \subseteq \bigcap_{t=0}^{\infty} \bigcup_{n=t}^{\infty} S[d_n]. \tag{4.6}$$

Some notation will be helpful. For $n \in \mathbf{N}$, let

$$B_n = \{ \pi \in \{0,1\}^{\leq 2^n - f(n)} \mid U(\pi, n) \in \{0,1\}^{2^n} \text{ in } \leq 2^{cn} \text{ space } \}. \tag{4.7}$$

For $n \in \mathbf{N}$ and $\pi \in B_n$, let

$$Z_{n,\pi} = \bigcup_{|z|=2^n-1} C_{zU(\pi,n)}.$$

(Thus $Z_{n,\pi}$ is the set of all languages A such that $U(\pi,n)$ is the 2^n-bit characteristic string of $A_{=n}$.) For $n \in \mathbf{N}$ and $w \in \{0,1\}^*$, let

$$\sigma(n,w) = \sum_{\pi \in B_n} \Pr(Z_{n,\pi}|C_w), \tag{4.8}$$

where the conditional probabilities $\Pr(Z_{n,\pi}|C_w) = \Pr_A[A \in Z_{n,\pi}|A \in C_w]$ are computed according to the random experiment in which a language $A \subseteq \{0,1\}^*$ is chosen probabilistically, using an independent toss of a fair coin to decide membership of each string in A. Finally, define the function $d : \mathbf{N} \times \{0,1\}^* \to [0,\infty)$ as follows. (In all three clauses, $n \in \mathbf{N}$, $w \in \{0,1\}^*$, and $b \in \{0,1\}$.)

 (i) If $0 \le |w| < 2^n - 1$, then $d_n(w) = 2^{1-f(n)}$.
 (ii) If $2^n - 1 \le |w| < 2^{n+1} - 1$, then $d_n(wb) = d_n(w)\frac{\sigma(n,wb)}{\sigma(n,w)}$.
(iii) If $|w| \ge 2^{n+1} - 1$, then $d_n(wb) = d_n(w)$.

(The condition $\sigma(n,w) = 0$ can only occur if $d_n(w) = 0$, in which case we understand clause (ii) to mean that $d_n(wb) = 0$.)

It is clear from (4.8) that

$$\sigma(n,w) = \frac{\sigma(n,w0) + \sigma(n,w1)}{2}$$

for all $n \in \mathbf{N}$ and $w \in \{0,1\}^*$. It follows by a routine induction on the definition of d that d is a 1-DS. It is also routine to check that d is pspace-computable. (The crucial point here is that we are only required to perform computations of the type (4.8) when $|w| \ge 2^n - 1$, so the 2^{cn} space bound of (4.7) is polynomial in $|w|$.) Since $\sum_{n=0}^{\infty} 2^{-f(n)}$ is p-convergent, it is immediate from clause (i) that (4.5) holds. All that remains, then, is to verify (4.6).

For each language $A \subseteq \{0,1\}^*$, let

$$I_A = \{n \in \mathbf{N} \mid KS^{2^{cn}}(A_{=n}) \le 2^n - f(n)\}.$$

Fix a language A for a moment and let $n \in I_A$. Then there exists $\pi_0 \in B_n$ such that $A \in Z_{n,\pi_0}$. Fix such a program π_0 and let $x,y \in \{0,1\}^*$ be the characterstic strings of $A_{<n}$, $A_{\le n}$, respectively. (Thus $|x| = 2^n - 1$, $|y| = 2^{n+1} - 1$, and $y = xU(\pi_0,n)$.) The definition of d tells us that $d_n(y)$ is $d_n(x)$ times a telescoping product, i.e.,

$$\begin{aligned}
d_n(y) &= d_n(x) \prod_{i=0}^{2^n-1} \frac{\sigma(n,y[0..2^n+i])}{\sigma(n,y[0..2^n-1+i])} \\
&= d_n(x)\frac{\sigma(n,y)}{\sigma(n,x)} \\
&= 2^{1-f(n)}\frac{\sigma(n,y)}{\sigma(n,x)}.
\end{aligned} \tag{4.9}$$

Since $C_y \subseteq Z_{n,\pi_0}$, we have

$$\sigma(n, y) = \sum_{\pi \in B_n} \Pr(Z_{n,\pi}|C_y) \geq \Pr(Z_{n,\pi_0}|C_y) = 1. \tag{4.10}$$

For each $\pi \in B_n$, the events C_x and $Z_{n,\pi}$ are independent, so

$$\begin{aligned}
\sigma(n, x) &= \sum_{\pi \in B_n} \Pr(Z_{n,\pi}|C_x) \\
&= \sum_{\pi \in B_n} \Pr(Z_{n,\pi}) \\
&= |B_n| 2^{-2^n} \\
&< 2^{1-f(n)}.
\end{aligned} \tag{4.11}$$

By (4.9), (4.10), and (4.11), we have $d_n(y) > 1$. It follows that $A \in C_y \subseteq S[d_n]$. Since $n \in I_A$ is arbitrary here, we have shown that $A \in S[d_n]$ for all $A \subseteq \{0,1\}^*$ and $n \in I_A$. It follows that, for all $A \subseteq \{0,1\}^*$,

$$\begin{aligned}
A \in X^c &\Rightarrow |I_A| = \infty \\
&\Rightarrow A \in S[d_n] \text{ i.o.} \\
&\Rightarrow A \in \bigcap_{t=0}^{\infty} \bigcup_{n=t}^{\infty} S[d_n],
\end{aligned}$$

i.e., (4.6) holds. This completes the proof.

Corollary 7. *Let $c \in \mathbf{N}$ and $\epsilon > 0$. If*

$$X = \{A \subseteq \{0,1\}^* | KS^{2^{cn}}(A_{=n}) > 2^n - n^\epsilon \text{ a.e.}\},$$

then $\mu_{\mathrm{pspace}}(X) = \mu(X|\mathrm{ESPACE}) = 1$.

Proof. Routine calculus shows that the series $\sum_{n=0}^{\infty} 2^{-n^\epsilon}$ is p-convergent. $\quad\square$

Corollary 7 is clearly a substantial improvement of Theorem 3(a). We will exploit this improvement in the following two sections.

5 Complexity Cores

A complexity core for a language A is a fixed set $K \subseteq \{0,1\}^*$ such that every machine consistent with A fails to decide efficiently on almost all inputs from K. In this section we review this notion carefully and prove that upper bounds on the size of complexity cores for a language A imply corresponding upper bounds on the space-bounded Kolmogorov complexity of A.

Given a machine M and an input $x \in \{0,1\}^*$, we write $M(x) = 1$ if M accepts x, $M(x) = 0$ if M rejects x, and $M(x) = \bot$ in any other case (i.e., if M fails to halt or M halts without deciding x). If $M(x) \in \{0,1\}$, we write $space_M(x)$ for the number of tape cells used in the computation of $M(x)$. If $M(x) = \bot$, we define $space_M(x) = \infty$. We partially order the set $\{0,1,\bot\}$ by $\bot < 0$ and $\bot < 1$, with 0 and 1 incomparable. A machine M is *consistent* with a language $A \subseteq \{0,1\}^*$ if $M(x) \leq [\![x \in A]\!]$ for all $x \in \{0,1\}^*$.

Definition 8. Let $s : \mathbf{N} \to \mathbf{N}$ be a space bound and let $A, K \subseteq \{0,1\}^*$. Then K is a DSPACE($s(n)$)-*complexity core* of A if, for every $c \in \mathbf{N}$ and every machine M that is consistent with A, the "fast set"

$$F = \{x \mid space_M(x) \le c \cdot s(|x|) + c\}$$

satisfies $|F \cap K| < \infty$. (By our definition of $space_M(x)$, $M(x) \in \{0,1\}$ for all $x \in F$. Thus F is the set of all strings that M "decides efficiently".)

Note that every subset of a DSPACE($s(n)$)-complexity core of A is a DSPACE($s(n)$)-complexity core of A. Note also that, if $t(n) = O(s(n))$, then every DSPACE($s(n)$)-complexity core of A is a DSPACE($t(n)$)-complexity core of A.

Remark. Definition 8 quantifies over all machines consistent with A, while the standard definition of complexity cores (cf. [BDG90]) quantifies only over machines that *decide A*. This difference renders Definition 8 stronger than the standard definition when A is not recursive. For example, consider *tally* languages (i.e., languages $A \subseteq \{0\}^*$). Under Definition 8, every DSPACE(n)-complexity core K of every tally language must satisfy $|K \setminus \{0\}^*| < \infty$. However, under the standard definition, *every* set $K \subseteq \{0,1\}^*$ is *vacuously* a complexity core for *every* nonrecursive language (tally or otherwise). Thus by quantifying over all machines consistent with A, Definition 8 makes the notion of complexity core meaningful for nonrecursive languages A. This enables one to eliminate the extraneous hypothesis that A is recursive from several results. In some cases (e.g., the fact that A is P-bi-immune if and only if $\{0,1\}^*$ is a P-complexity core for A [BS85]), this improvement is of little interest. However in §6 below, we show that *every* $\le_m^P$-hard language H for ESPACE has unusually small complexity cores, hence unusually low space-bounded Kolmogorov complexity. This upper bound holds regardless of whether H is recursive.

It should also be noted that standard existence theorems on complexity cores (e.g., every language $A \notin$ P has an infinite P-complexity core [Lyn75]; every $\le_m^P$-hard language for E has a dense P-complexity core [OS86]) remain true under Definition 8. Thus no harm is done by quantifying over all machines consistent with A.

Intuitively, a language is complex if it has very large complexity cores. The converse implication, that a language is simple if it does not have large complexity cores, is supported by the following technical result.

Theorem 9. *Let $A \subseteq \{0,1\}^*$, $\epsilon > 0$, $b > c > 0$, and $g : \mathbf{N} \to [0,\infty)$. If every DSPACE($2^{cn}$)-complexity core K of A has density $|K_{=n}| \le 2^n - g(n)$ i.o., then $KS^{2^{bn}}(A_{=n}) < 2^n - n^{-\epsilon}g(n) + 3\epsilon \log n$ i.o.*

Proof. Let $A \subseteq \{0,1\}^*$, $\epsilon > 0$, and $b > c > 0$. Let $k = \lceil \frac{1}{\epsilon} \rceil$, fix a, d such that $b > a > d > c$, and let $M_0, M_1, M_2, \ldots$ be a standard enumeration of the deterministic Turing machines. For each $m \in \mathbf{N}$, define the sets

$$F_m = \{x \,|\, space_{M_m}(x) \le 2^{d|x|}\},$$
$$B_m = F_m \setminus \{0,1\}^{\le m^k},$$
$$B = \bigcup_{cons(m,A)} B_m,$$
$$K = \{0,1\}^* \setminus B,$$

where the predicate $cons(m, A)$ asserts that M_m is consistent with A. Note that, if M_m is a machine that is consistent with A, then $F_m \cap K = F_m \setminus B \subseteq F_m \setminus B_m \subseteq \{0,1\}^{\le m^k}$, so $|F_m \cap K| < \infty$. Thus K is a DSPACE(2^{cn})-complexity core for A.

Let

$$S = \left\{ n \,\Big|\, |K_{=n}| \le 2^n - g(n) \right\} = \left\{ n \,\Big|\, |B_{=n}| \ge g(n) \right\}.$$

Then, for each $n \in S$, we have

$$g(n) \le |B_{=n}| = |(\bigcup_{cons(m,A)} B_m)_{=n}|$$
$$\le \sum_{cons(m,A)} |(B_m)_{=n}|$$
$$= \sum_{(m^k < n) \wedge (cons(m,A))} |(B_m)_{=n}|$$
$$\le \sum_{(0 \le m < n^\epsilon) \wedge (cons(m,A))} |(B_m)_{=n}|$$
$$\le \sum_{(0 \le m < n^\epsilon) \wedge (cons(m,A))} |(F_m)_{=n}|$$

and there are $\le n^\epsilon$ terms in this last sum, so there exists $0 \le m < n^\epsilon$ such that M_m is consistent with A and $|(F_m)_{=n}| \ge n^{-\epsilon} g(n)$.

Now let M be a machine that implements the algorithm of Figure 1 with input $(\langle \beta(m), y \rangle, n)$, where $y \in \{0,1\}^*$ and $\beta(m)$ is the binary representation of a natural number m. (Let $N = 2^n$ and let $w_0, ..., w_{N-1}$ be the lexicographic enumeration of $\{0,1\}^n$. We use the symbol $\perp$ for a bit of z that has not yet been defined. For a string $y \ne \lambda$, $head(y)$ is the first bit of y and $tail(y)$ is the rest of y.) Since $a > d$, it is clear that M can be designed so that $M(\langle \beta(m), y \rangle, n)$ uses $\le 2^{an}$ workspace. For each $n \in S$, choose $m \in \mathbf{N}$ and $y \in \{0,1\}^*$ such that $0 \le m < n^\epsilon$, M_m is consistent with A, $|(F_m)_{=n}| \ge n^{-\epsilon} g(n)$, and y consists of the $2^n - |(F_m)_{=n}|$ successive bits $[\![w_i \in A]\!]$ for $w_i \in \{0,1\}^n \setminus F_m$. Then $M(\langle \beta(m), y \rangle, n)$ is the 2^n-bit characteristic string of $A_{=n}$, so

$$KS_M^{2^{an}}(A_{=n}) \le |\langle \beta(m), y \rangle|$$
$$= |y| + 2|\beta(m)| + 2$$
$$\le 2^n - |(F_m)_{=n}| + 2 \log m + 3$$
$$\le 2^n - n^{-\epsilon} g(n) + 2\epsilon \log n + 3.$$

```
        begin
            z := ⊥^N;
            for i := 0 to N − 1 do
            begin
                    Simulate M_m(w_i) as long as this uses ≤ 2^{dn} space.
                    if this simulation accepts or rejects
                        then set z[i] := 1 or z[i] := 0, respectively
                        else (z[i], y) := (head(y), tail(y))
            end;
            output z;
        end M.
```

Fig. 1. Algorithm for proof of Theorem 9.

It follows that there is a constant $c_M \in \mathbf{N}$ such that, for all $n \in S$,

$$KS^{2^{bn}}(A_{=n}) \leq 2^n - n^{-\epsilon}g(n) + 2\epsilon \log n + 3 + c_M.$$

Hence,

$$KS^{2^{bn}}(A_{=n}) \leq 2^n - n^{-\epsilon}g(n) + 3\epsilon \log n. \tag{5.1}$$

for all but finitely many $n \in S$.

If the hypothesis of Theorem 9 holds, then S is infinite, so (5.1) holds i.o.

Since almost every language in ESPACE has high space-bounded Kolmogorov complexity almost everywhere, Theorem 9 allows us to conclude that almost every language in ESPACE has very large complexity cores.

Theorem 10. *Fix real constants $c > 0$ and $\epsilon > 0$. Let Y be the set of all languages A such that A has a $DSPACE(2^{cn})$-complexity core K with $|K_{=n}| > 2^n - n^\epsilon$ a.e. Then $\mu_{\mathrm{pspace}}(Y) = \mu(Y|ESPACE) = 1$.*

Proof. Let c, ϵ and Y be as given. Assume that $A \notin Y$. Then every $DSPACE(2^{cn})$-complexity core K of A has $|K_{=n}| \leq 2^n - n^\epsilon$ i.o. Since $\frac{\epsilon}{2} > 0$, it follows by Theorem 9 that

$$KS^{2^{(c+1)n}}(A_{=n}) < 2^n - n^{\frac{\epsilon}{2}} + 2\epsilon \log n \text{ i.o.}$$

Since $n^{\frac{\epsilon}{2}} > n^{\frac{\epsilon}{4}} + 2\epsilon \log n$ a.e., it follows that

$$KS^{2^{(c+1)n}}(A_{=n}) < 2^n - n^{\frac{\epsilon}{4}} \text{ i.o.}$$

Taking the contrapositive, this argument shows that $X \subseteq Y$, where

$$X = \{A \subseteq \{0,1\}^* | KS^{2^{(c+1)n}}(A_{=n}) > 2^n - n^{\frac{\epsilon}{4}} \text{ a.e.}\}.$$

It follows by Corollary 7 that $\mu_{\mathrm{pspace}}(Y) = \mu(Y|ESPACE) = 1$.

Corollary 11. *For every $c > 0$, almost every language in ESPACE has a co-sparse $DSPACE(2^{cn})$-complexity core.*

6 The Distribution of Hardness

In this section we use the results of §§4-5 to investigate the complexity and distribution of the $\leq_m^P$-hard languages for ESPACE. From a technical standpoint, the main result of this section is Theorem 12, which says that every $\leq_m^P$-hard language for ESPACE is DSPACE(2^n)-decidable on a dense, DSPACE(2^n)-decidable set of inputs.

Two simple notations will be useful in the proof of Theorem 12. First, the *nonreduced image* of a language $S \subseteq \{0,1\}^*$ under a function $f : \{0,1\}^* \to \{0,1\}^*$ is

$$f^{\geq}(S) = \{f(x) \mid x \in S \text{ and } |f(x)| \geq |x|\}.$$

Note that

$$f^{\geq}(f^{-1}(S)) = S \cap f^{\geq}(\{0,1\}^*)$$

for all f and S.

The *collision set* of a function $f : \{0,1\}^* \to \{0,1\}^*$ is

$$C_f = \{x \mid (\exists y < x)f(x) = f(y)\}.$$

(Here, we are using the standard ordering $s_0 < s_1 < s_2 < ...$ of $\{0,1\}^*$.) Note that f is one-to-one if and only if $C_f = \emptyset$. Also,

$$|S| \leq |f(S)| + |C_f|$$

holds for every set $S \subseteq \{0,1\}^*$.

A language $A \subseteq \{0,1\}^*$ is *incompressible* by $\leq_m^P$-reductions if $|C_f| < \infty$ for every $\leq_m^P$-reduction f of A.

Theorem 12. *For every $\leq_m^P$-hard language H for ESPACE, there exist $B, D \in$ DSPACE(2^n) such that D is dense and $B = H \cap D$.*

Proof. By a construction of Meyer[Mey77], there is a language $A \in$ DSPACE(2^n) that is incompressible by $\leq_m^P$-reductions. For the sake of completeness, we review the construction of A at the end of this proof. First, however, we use A to prove Theorem 12.

Let H be $\leq_m^P$-hard for ESPACE. Then there is a $\leq_m^P$-reduction f of A to H. Let $B = f^{\geq}(A), D = f^{\geq}(\{0,1\}^*)$. Since $A \in$ DSPACE(2^n) and $f \in PF$, it is clear that $B, D \in$ DSPACE(2^n).

Fix a polynomial q and a real number $\epsilon > 0$ such that $|f(x)| \leq q(|x|)$ for all $x \in \{0,1\}^*$ and $q(n^{2\epsilon}) < n$ a.e. Let $W = \{x \mid |f(x)| < |x|\}$. Then, for all sufficiently large $n \in \mathbf{N}$, writing $m = \lfloor n^{2\epsilon} \rfloor$, we have

$$\begin{aligned}
f(\{0,1\}^{\leq m}) \setminus \{0,1\}^{<m} &\subseteq f(\{0,1\}^{\leq m}) \setminus f(W_{\leq m}) \\
&\subseteq f^{\geq}(\{0,1\}^{\leq m}) \\
&\subseteq D_{\leq q(m)} \\
&\subseteq D_{\leq n},
\end{aligned}$$

whence

$$|D_{\leq n}| \geq |f(\{0,1\}^{\leq m})| - |\{0,1\}^{<m}|$$
$$\geq |\{0,1\}^{\leq m}| - |C_f| - |\{0,1\}^{<m}|$$
$$= 2^m - |C_f|.$$

Since $|C_f| < \infty$, it follows that $|D_{\leq n}| > 2^{n^\epsilon}$ for all sufficiently large n. Thus D is dense.

Finally, note that $B = f^{\geq}(A) = f^{\geq}(f^{-1}(H)) = H \cap f^{\geq}(\{0,1\}^*) = H \cap D$. This completes the proof of Theorem 12.

We now describe Meyer's construction of the language A. It is well-known that there is a function $g \in \mathrm{DTIMEF}(n^{\log n})$ that is universal for PF in the sense that

$$\mathrm{PF} = \{g_k | k \in \mathbf{N}\}.$$

(Recall that g_k is defined by $g_k(x) = g(\langle 0^k, x \rangle)$ for all $x \in \{0,1\}^*$.) Fix such a function g. Let $A = L(M)$, where M is a machine that implements the algorithm

```
begin
      input x ;
      R := ∅; S := ∅;
      for n := 0 to |x| do
      begin
            R := R ∪ {n};
            if there exists (k, y, z) ∈ R × {0,1}^n × {0,1}^{≤n}
                such that z < y and g_k(y) = g_k(z) then
            begin
                  find the lexicographically first such (k, y, z);
                  if z ∉ S then S := S ∪ {y};
                  R := R \ {k}
            end
      end;
      if x ∈ S then accept else reject
end M.
```

Fig. 2. Meyer's construction (for proof of Theorem 12).

in Figure 2. It is clear by inspection that $A \in \mathrm{DSPACE}(2^n)$. To see that A is incompressible by $\leq_m^P$-reductions, suppose that $f \in \mathrm{PF}$ and $|C_f| = \infty$. It suffices to show that f is not a $\leq_m^P$-reduction of A. Fix $k \in \mathbf{N}$ such that $f = g_k$. Then there is some $n \in \mathbf{N}$ such that, on input $x = 0^n$, M finds a triple (k, y, z) on cycle n of the for-loop. We then have $f(y) = g_k(y) = g_k(z) = f(z)$ and $y \in A \iff z \notin A$, so $f^{-1}(f(A)) \neq A$, so f is not a $\leq_m^P$-reduction of A.

We now use Theorem 12 to prove our upper bound on the size of complexity cores for hard languages.

Theorem 13. *Every DSPACE(2^n)-complexity core of every $\leq_m^P$-hard language for ESPACE has a dense complement.*

Proof. Let H be $\leq_m^P$-hard for ESPACE, and let K be a DSPACE(2^n)- complexity core of H. Choose B, D for H as in Theorem 12. Fix machines M_B, and M_D that decide B and D respectively, with $space_{M_B}(x) = O(2^{|x|})$ and $space_{M_D}(x) = O(2^{|x|})$. Let M be a machine that implements the following algorithm.

begin
    input x;
    if $M_D(x)$ accepts
        then simulate $M_B(x)$
        else run forever
end M.

Then $x \in D \Rightarrow M(x) = [\![x \in B]\!] = [\![x \in H \cap D]\!] = [\![x \in H]\!]$ and $x \notin D \Rightarrow M(x) = \perp \leq [\![x \in H]\!]$, so M is consistent with H. Also, there is a constant $c \in \mathbf{N}$ such that for all $x \in D$,

$$space_M(x) \leq c2^n + c.$$

Since K is a DSPACE(2^n)-complexity core of H, it follows that $K \cap D$ is finite. But D is dense, so this implies that $D \setminus K$ is dense, whence K^c is dense.

Our upper bound on the size of complexity cores now yields an upper bound on the space-bounded Kolmogorov complexity of hard languages.

Theorem 14. *For every $\leq_m^P$-hard language H for ESPACE, there exists $\epsilon > 0$ such that*
$$KS^{2^{2^n}}(H_{=n}) < 2^n - 2^{n^\epsilon} \quad i.o.$$

Proof. Let H be $\leq_m^P$-hard for ESPACE. By Theorem 13, there exists $\epsilon > 0$ such that every DSPACE(2^n)-complexity core K of H has density $|K_{=n}| \leq 2^n - 2^{n^{2\epsilon}}$ i.o. It follows by Theorem 9 that $KS^{2^{2^n}}(H_{=n}) < 2^n - n^{-1}2^{n^{2\epsilon}} + 3\log n$ i.o. Since $n^{-1}2^{n^{2\epsilon}} > 2^{n^\epsilon} + 3\log n$ a.e., this implies that $KS^{2^{2^n}}(H_{=n}) < 2^n - 2^{n^\epsilon}$ i.o.

Theorems 13 and 14 give upper bounds on the complexity of hard languages. All that remains is to observe that it is unusual for languages in ESPACE to satisfy these bounds:

Theorem 15. *Let $\mathcal{H}$, $\mathcal{C}$ be the sets of languages that are $\leq_m^P$-hard, $\leq_m^P$-complete for ESPACE, respectively. (Thus, $\mathcal{C} = \mathcal{H} \cap ESPACE$.) Then $\mathcal{H}$ has pspace-measure 0, so $\mathcal{C}$ is a measure 0 subset of ESPACE.*

Proof. By Theorem 14, $\mathcal{H} \cap \{A \subseteq \{0,1\}^* \mid KS^{2^{2^n}}(A_{=n}) > 2^n - \sqrt{n} \text{ a.e.}\} = \emptyset$, so this follows from Corollary 7.

7 Conclusion

Very roughly speaking, our results (together with earlier work of [OS86, Huy86]) admit the following simple summary. We use $KS(A_{=n})$ and $|K_{=n}|$ as measures of the complexity of a language A, where K is a "largest" complexity core for A. These measures *roughly* satisfy the condition $0 \leq KS(A_{=n}) \leq |K_{=n}| \leq 2^n$. In both measures, *almost every* language in ESPACE has complexity $\approx 2^n$ for almost every n. In both measures, *every hard* language for ESPACE has complexity between 2^{n^ϵ} and $2^n - 2^{n^\epsilon}$ for infinitely many n. In fact [JL92], these bounds are tight.

Acknowledgment

We thank Osamu Watanabe and two anonymous reviewers for suggestions that have improved the exposition of this paper.

References

[All89] E. W. Allender. Some consequences of the existence of pseudorandom generators. *Journal of Computer and System Sciences* 39:101–124, 1989.

[AR88] E. W. Allender and R. Rubinstein. P-printable sets. *SIAM Journal on Computing* 17:1193–1202 ,1988.

[AW90] E. W. Allender and O. Watanabe. Kolmogorov complexity and degrees of tally sets. *Information and Computation* 86:160–178, 1990.

[Amb86] K. Ambos-Spies. Randomness, relativizations, and polynomial reducibilities. In *Proceedings of the First Annual Structure in Complexity Theory Conference*, pages 23–34, 1986.

[BB86] J. L. Balcázar and R. Book. Sets with small generalized Kolmogorov complexity. *Acta Informatica* 23:679–688, 1986.

[BDG88] J. L. Balcázar, J. Díaz, and J. Gabarró. *Structural Complexity I*, Springer-Verlag, 1988.

[BDG90] J. L. Balcázar, J. Díaz, and J. Gabarró. *Structural Complexity II*, Springer-Verlag, 1990.

[BS85] J. L. Balcázar and U. Schöning. Bi-immune sets for complexity classes. *Mathematical Systems Theory* 18:1–10, 1985.

[Ber76] L. Berman. On the structure of complete sets: almost everywhere complexity and infinitely often speed-up. In *Proceedings of the 17th. IEEE Symp. of the Foundations of Computer Science*, pages 76–80, 1976.

[BH77] L. Berman and J. Hartmanis. On isomorphism and density of NP and other complete sets. *SIAM Journal on Computing* 6:305–322, 1977.

[BD87] R. Book and D.-Z. Du. The existence and density of generalized complexity cores. *Journal of the Association for Computing Machinery* 34:718–730, 1987.

[BDR88] R. Book, D.-Z Du, and D. Russo. On polynomial and generalized complexity cores. In *Proceedings of the Third Structure in Complexity Theory Conference*, pages 236–250, 1988.

[Cha66] G. J. Chaitin. On the length of programs for computing finite binary sequences. *Journal of the Association for Computing Machinery* 13:547–569, 1966.

[Du85]   D.-Z. Du. Generalized complexity cores and levelability of intractable sets. Ph.D. dissertation, University of California, Santa Barbara, CA. 1985.

[DB89]   D.-Z. Du and R. Book. On inefficient special cases of *NP*-complete problems. *Theoretical Computer Science* 63:239–252, 1989.

[ESY85]   S. Even, A. Selman, and Y. Yacobi. Hard core theorems for complexity classes. *Journal of the Association for Computing Machinery* 35:205–217, 1985.

[GJ79]   M. R. Garey and D. S. Johnson. *Computers and Intractability: A Guide to the Theory of NP-completeness*, W.H. Freeman and Company, 1979.

[Har83]   J. Hartmanis. Generalized Kolmogorov complexity and the structure of feasible computations. In *Proceedings of the 24th IEEE Symposium on the Foundations of Computer Science*, pages 439–445, 1983.

[HY84]   J. Hartmanis and Y. Yesha. Computation times of NP sets of different densities. *Theoretical Computer Science* 34:17–32, 1984.

[Huy86]   D. T. Huynh. Resource-bounded Kolmogorov complexity of hard languages. In *Proceedings of the First Annual Structure in Complexity Theory Conference*, pages 184–195, 1986.

[Huy87]   D. T. Huynh. On solving hard problems by polynomial-size circuits. *Information Processing Letters* 24:171–176, 1987.

[JL92]   D. W. Juedes and J. H. Lutz. The complexity and distribution of hard problems. in preparation.

[Kan82]   R. Kannan. Circuit-size lower bounds and non-reducibility to sparse sets. *Information and Control* 55:40–56, 1982.

[Kar72]   R. Karp. Reducibility among combinatorial problems. In *Complexity of Computer Computations*. Ed. R. E. Miller, and J. W. Thatcher, 85–104. New York: Plenum Press, 1972.

[KL80]   R. M. Karp and R. J. Lipton. Some connections between nonuniform and uniform complexity classes. In *Proceedings of the 12th ACM Symposium on Theory of Computing*, pages 302–309, 1980. Also published as Turing machines that take advice. *L'Enseignement Mathematique* 28:191–209, 1982.

[Ko86]   K. Ko. On the notion of infinite pseudorandom sequences. *Theoretical Computer Science* 48:9–33, 1986.

[KM81]   K. Ko, and D. Moore. Completeness, approximation, and density. *SIAM Journal on Computing* 10:787–796, 1981.

[Kol65]   A. N. Kolmogorov. Three approaches to the quantitative definition of 'information'. *Problems of Information Transmission* 1:1–7, 1965.

[Lev84]   L. A. Levin. Randomness conservation inequalities; information and independence in mathematical theories. *Information and Control* 61:15–37, 1984.

[Lon86]   L. Longpré. Resource bounded Kolmogorov complexity, a link between computational complexity and information theory. Ph.D. thesis, Cornell University, 1986. Technical Report TR-86-776.

[Lup58]   O. B. Lupanov. On the synthesis of contact networks. *Dokl. Akad. Nauk SSSR* 19:23–26, 1958.

[Lut90]   J. H. Lutz. Category and measure in complexity classes. *SIAM Journal on Computing* 19:1100–1131, 1990.

[Lut91]   J. H. Lutz. An upward measure separation theorem. *Theoretical Computer Science* 81:127–135, 1991.

[Lut92a] J. H. Lutz. Almost everywhere high nonuniform complexity. *Journal of Computer and System Sciences* 44, 1992, to appear.

[Lut92b] J. H. Lutz. Resource-bounded measure. in preparation.

[Lyn75] N. Lynch. On reducibility to complex or sparse sets. *Journal of the Association for Computing Machinery* 22:341–345, 1975.

[Mar71] P. Martin-Löf. Complexity oscillations in infinite binary sequences. *Zeitschrift für Wahrscheinlichkeitstheory und Verwandte Gebiete* 19:225-230, 1971.

[May91] E. Mayordomo. Almost every set in exponential time is P-bi-immune. In *Proceedings of the Seventeenth International Symposium on Mathematical Foundations of Computer Science*, Springer–Verlag, 1992, to appear.

[Mey77] A. R. Meyer. reported in [BH77].

[MS72] A. R. Meyer and L. Stockmeyer. The equivalence problem for regular expressions with squaring requires exponential space. In *Proceedings of the 13th IEEE Symposium on Switching and Automata Theory*, pages 125–129, 1972.

[NW88] N. Nisan and A. Wigderson. Hardness vs. randomness. In *Proceedings of the 29th IEEE Symposium on Foundations of Computer Science*, pages 2–11, 1988.

[Orp86] P. Orponen. A classification of complexity core lattices. *Theoretical Computer Science* 70:121–130, 1986.

[OS86] P. Orponen and U. Schöning. The density and complexity of polynomial cores for intractable sets. *Information and Control* 70:54–68, 1986.

[RO87] D. A. Russo and P. Orponen On P-subset structures. *Mathematical Systems Theory* 20:129–136, 1987.

[Sha49] C. E. Shannon. The synthesis of two-terminal switching circuits. *Bell System Technical Journal* 28:59–98, 1949.

[Sip83] M. Sipser. A complexity-theoretic approach to randomness. In *Proceedings of the 15th ACM Symposium of the Theory of Computing*, pages 330–335, 1983.

[Sol64] R. J. Solomonoff. A formal theory of inductive inference. *Information and Control* 7:1–22,224–254, 1964.

[SC89] L. Stockmeyer and A. K. Chandra. Provably difficult combinatorial games. *SIAM Journal on Computing* 8:151–174, 1979.

[Weg87] I. Wegener. *The Complexity of Boolean Functions.* (Wiley–Teubner series in computer science), Stuttgart: Wiley–Teubner, 1987.

[Wil85] C. B. Wilson. Relativized circuit complexity. *Journal of Computer and System Sciences* 31:169–181, 1985.

[Ye90] H. Ye. Complexity cores for P/poly. submitted.

Resource Bounded Kolmogorov Complexity and Statistical Tests

Luc Longpré

College of Computer Science
Northeastern University
Boston, MA 02115, USA
e-mail: luc@corwin.ccs.northeastern.edu

Abstract. This paper investigates the statistical properties of resource bounded Kolmogorov-random strings. In an attempt to define random sequences, Martin-Löf has shown that the Kolmogorov-random strings (strings with no short description) possess all the statistical properties of random strings. We look at the statistical properties of *resource bounded* Kolmogorov-random strings. For space bounds, we show that there is a direct relation between the space bound on the Kolmogorov randomness classes and the space required to check a statistical property. The problem is still open for time bounds. We then relate this notion of random sequences to Yao's definition of secure pseudo random number generators.

1 Introduction

Before looking at Martin-Löf's results, let's review briefly the attempts to define random sequences. For a more detailed discussion of the history of theories of probability and random sequences, see [Fin73, vL87, LV88, LV91] (from which this overview is inspired).

The concept of randomness comes up in various forms in mathematics and computer science. The formalization of the concept has resulted in various theories of probability, that differ according to their domains of application and their goal. These theories have also gone through evolution with time and new discoveries.

There have been many attempts at formalizing probability. Kolmogorov [Kol33] (see the English translation in [Kol56]) developed in 1933 his axiomatic quantitative probability, which is since widely accepted. A quantitative probability is one that provides a probability measure predicate P that measures the probability of every possible event. Kolmogorov's formulation consists of a probability space $(\Omega, \mathcal{F}, P)$, where Ω is the sample space, $\mathcal{F}$ is a σ-algebra of selected subsets of Ω, and P the probability measure. His axioms are as follows:

1. Unit normalization: $P(\Omega) = 1$.
2. Nonnegativity: $(\forall F \in \mathcal{F})P(F) \geq 0$.

3. Finite additivity: $F_1, ..., F_n \in \mathcal{F}$ and pairwise disjoint imply $P(\cup_{i=1}^n F_i) = \Sigma_{i=1}^n P(F_i)$.

4. Continuity: $(\forall i) F_i \supseteq F_{i+1}$ and $\cap_{i=1}^\infty F_i = \emptyset$ implies $\lim_{i \to \infty} P(F_i) = 0$.

Since probability is supposed to model a physical phenomenon or describe a law of nature (at least initially), many researchers have tried to interpret the model in terms of the property of random experiments. In particular, von Mises was interested in the applicability of probability to real world phenomena. He suggested that the study of probability is intricately tied to the study of random sequences [vM19, vM39]. He considered the study of repeating an experiment, each trial having a finite number of possible outcomes, and each trial being unrelated (see [vMG64]). He introduced a field of events $\mathcal{V}$ that describes the possible results of this infinite number of experiments. If Ω is the σ-algebra as defined by Kolmogorov, then consider the set of all infinite sequences of elements of Ω. A cylinder over this set is a set of infinite sequences determined by a finite number of positions. For example, all sequences that have a 0 in the first position and a 1 in the 5th position. The field $\mathcal{V}$ is the closure of the set of all cylinders under (finite) unions and complements, and under the following limiting property:

> If V is such that there exist infinite sequences L_i and U_i having the following properties:
> 1. $(\forall n) L_n \subseteq V \subseteq U_n$,
> 2. $\lim_{n \to \infty} [P(U_n) - P(L_n)] = 0$,
> then $V \in \mathcal{V}$.

The consideration of infinite sequences and the desire to apply the theory to real random phenomena led to the frequency concept of probability. If an experiment is performed a finite number of times, there will be a fluctuation in the relative frequency of outcomes. But, as the number of experiments grows, there seems to be a decrease in this fluctuation. From this, it is tempting to define probability as the limit of this relative frequency, as the number of experiments tends to infinity. This is called the frequentist's approach.

One problem arises from this approach when one tries to make statements about future outcomes of an experiment. The above definition says nothing about the rate of convergence. Perhaps we would like to say that the frequency will be ϵ-close to the limiting frequency after some number of trials. But if we want to include the rate of convergence in the definition of probability, it seems inevitable that the definition becomes circular.

In 1919, von Mises [vM19] addresses this problem when he introduced his definition of random sequences, which he calls *collectives*. Following the notation in [vMG64],

Definition 1. A *collective* $K(\Phi, \Omega)$ is an infinite sequence S of elements of Ω and a family Φ of place-selection functions that is closed under composition such that

1. $(\forall \omega_i \in \Omega)$, the number of occurrences of ω_i in the first n terms of S tends to p_i as n tends to infinity.

2. $\Sigma_{i=1}^{\infty} p_i = 1$.

3. If we generate an infinite subsequence S' from S by means of any place selection $\phi \in \Phi$, then S' satisfies 1. and 2. for the same $\{p_i\}$.

The third condition, intuitively says that there is no gambling strategy. It says that if we select any subsequence of S, using an admissible place selection, then the subsequence is also a collective with the same derived probabilities. In other words, assume a player is betting in fixed amounts, on the outcomes of the sequence, after seeing all the previous outcomes, then no gain can be obtained on the long run.

One problem with this definition is that the notion of *admissible* place selection has not been defined formally. Instead, von Mises gives examples of admissible place selection:

- choose those ω_n for which n is prime,
- choose those x_n which follow the word 010,
- toss a coin (independently) and choose ω_n if the nth toss yields heads.

While intuitively appealing, the lack of formality in von Mises' definition has fueled a stream of criticism against this theory. For example, we cannot accept as admissible the function that selects all the position for which the outcome is a 1. So, any formal definition should exclude those functions. Various authors have tried to provide formal definitions of admissible place selections. Wald [Wal38] proposed to restrict the set of place selection functions to any countable set of functions that on a string of length n representing the outcome of n experiments, decides whether to bet on the next experiment. He showed the existence of collectives under any such set of place selection functions. Church [Chu40] proposed to choose the set of recursive functions. This proposition offered a rigorous definition of random sequences. In addition, under this definition, the random sequences form a set of measure one. This goes along with the intuition that most sequences should be random.

But this definition turned out to be not good enough. For any countable set of place selections, Ville [Vil39] constructed a sequence which is a random sequence according to the definition, but has too much regularity to be called random. Up until now, there has been no acceptable way of giving a class of admissible place selections that provides a reasonable definition of random sequences, especially if we want to include as well the *random* place selections, as described by the original von Mises examples.

In 1966, Martin-Löf [ML66] gave a definition of random sequences based on Kolmogorov complexity and on statistical tests that did not have all the problems expressed above. He noticed that all statistical tests are effective. More precisely, if an infinite sequence fails the statistical test, then it fails on infinitely many increasing prefixes of the infinite sequence. So, we can define the set of infinite random sequences as the intersection of all sets of infinite sequences of measure one whose complement is recursively enumerable. This set is a set of measure one as well.

One important objection of all this work on infinite random sequences is exactly because they are infinite. After all, in practice, we never see infinite sequences, but only finite ones. In other words, if all we encounter in this world are finite sequences, why not base a theory of random sequences on finite sequences. An interesting aspect of the work of Kolmogorov [Kol63] and Martin-Löf [ML66] is that it also applies to finite sequences. Using Kolmogorov complexity, a *Kolmogorov-random* (K-random) string is a string of length n that cannot be printed by any program of size strictly less than n. The K-random strings have many nice properties of random strings. For example, given any portion of any K-random string, it is impossible to compute the remaining part of the string, because that would provide a short program to print the whole string. The K-random strings also have many other properties of random strings. In [ML66], Martin-Löf gave a definition of statistical test. His statistical tests have *levels of randomness*, and a finite sequence can pass or fail the test at various levels, with the restriction that fewer and fewer sequences fail the test as the level increases. He constructed a universal test and showed that the K-random strings possess all the computable statistical properties of the random strings by giving a direct relation between the length of the shortest program to print a string and the level of non-randomness given by this universal test.

After the evolution of computational complexity in the last 2 decades, it is important that we revisit those theories in the context of resource bounded environments. Looking back at infinite sequences, what is a reasonable definition of a space bounded or time bounded random sequence? Intuitively, there may be some sequences that are not random, but such that the non-randomness is so intricately buried that any space or time bounded process would fail to detect it. Research in this area is described in considerable details by Lutz in this book.

With respect to finite sequences, the same question arises. What is a good definition of a finite random sequence in a time or space bounded environments. Would all the Martin-Löf's theorems still hold? Can we still build a universal test? Can we use those new definitions in building pseudo random number generators?

It is impossible to use unbounded theories in building a pseudo random number generator, because it is undecidable whether or not a string is K-random. We can use time and space bounded Kolmogorov complexity (studied early on in [Har83, Sip83, Ko86, Lon86] and others) to define random sequences. Since these classes are decidable, answering this question is relevant to the theory of pseudo-random number generators, and gives more insight into related problems.

In this paper, we address those questions. Although historically, many researchers consider sequences of symbols from a finite alphabet, in the rest of this paper, we only consider sequences of 0 and 1. The theory developed could be extended to sequences of symbols from a finite alphabet. After reviewing careful definitions of Kolmogorov complexity classes used in this paper in section 2, we review the definition of Martin-Löf's statistical tests in section 3. We provide a simplified proof of Martin-Löf's result on finite random sequences in section 4. In section 5, we consider those notions in space bounded environments. We show on one hand that the Space Bounded Kolmogorov random (SBK-random) strings possess all the statistical properties that can be verified in less space. On the other hand, we show that if we allow a little more space, we can design a test that will single out some highly SBK-random strings (that are, of course, not K-random). Moreover, we build a space bounded universal test.

Although most of the problems are still open for time bounded environments, applying the techniques of section 5 to time bounds do give us some weak results. We give these results in section 6 and address the issue of whether the results could be strengthened.

In the last section we address the question of pseudo random number generators. Martin-Löf's notion of statistical tests is related to Yao's definition of a pseudo random number generator [Yao82]. We explore the relevance of our results to the construction of pseudo-random number generators.

2 Resource Bounded Kolmogorov Complexity

In this paper, we use several variants of Kolmogorov complexity functions and sets. The Kolmogorov complexity functions $K(\cdot)$ measure the Kolmogorov complexity of a finite string (the size of the shortest description of the string). The Kolmogorov complexity sets $K[\cdot]$ are sets containing all strings that have a bounded Kolmogorov complexity. We use in this paper classical and resource bounded complexity. We also use conditional Kolmogorov complexity.

Definition 2. For a Turing machine M_i and a finite string x, the Kolmogorov complexity of x with respect to M_i is defined as follows:

$$K_i(x) = \min\{l \mid (\exists y)[|y| = l) \text{ and } M_i(y) = x\} \ .$$

$K_i(x) = \infty$ if the above set is empty.

Definition 3. For a Turing machine M_i and a function $g(n) \geq 1$, the Kolmogorov complexity set based on M_i and g is defined as follows:

$$K_i[g(n)] = \{x \mid (\exists y)[|y| \leq g(|x|) \text{ and } M_i(y) = x\} \ .$$

Definition 4. For a Turing machine M_i, a space bound $S(n)$ and a string x, the space bounded Kolmogorov complexity of x is defined as follows:

$$KS_i(x, S(n)) = \min\{l \mid (\exists y)[|y| = l) \text{ and } M_i(y) = x,$$
$$\text{using at most } S(|x|) \text{ space}\} \ .$$

$K_i(x) = \infty$ if the above set is empty.

Definition 5. For a Turing machine M_i, a space bound $S(n)$ and a function $g(n) \geq 1$, the space bounded Kolmogorov complexity set is defined as follows:

$$KS_i[g(n), S(n)] = \{x \mid (\exists y)[|y| \leq g(|x|) \text{ and } M_i(y) = x,$$
$$\text{using at most } S(|x|) \text{ space}\} \ .$$

The function $KS_i(x, S(n))$ is the size of the smallest program that will print x, using at most $S(|x|)$ space to do so. The set $KS_i[g(n), S(n)]$ contains all the strings x that have a description of length $g(|x|)$, and for which we can recompute x within the space bound $S(|x|)$. The time bounded Kolmogorov complexity $KT(x, T(n))$ and sets $KT[g(n), T(n)]$ are defined similarly with a time bound instead of a space bound.

The main idea initially motivating those definitions is to measure randomness in finite sequences. If a pattern can be detected in a sequence, then there should be a description of the sequence that is shorter than the sequence itself. One drawback is that the definitions seem to depend on the choice of the Turing machine M_i. However, as observed by Solomonoff, Kolmogorov and Chaitin, if a universal Turing machine M_u is used in the definition, then the measure is nearly optimal:

Theorem 6 (Invariance Theorem [Sol64, Kol65, Cha69]).
There is a Turing machine M_u which is nearly optimal, in the sense that

$$(\forall i)(\exists c)[K_i[g(n)] \subseteq K_u[g(n) + c]] \ .$$

Hartmanis observed that if a space or time efficient universal Turing machine is used, then the invariance theorem still holds with time and space bounded Kolmogorov complexity:

Theorem 7 (Invariance Theorem, space bounded variant [Har83]).
There is a Turing machine M_u which is nearly optimal, in the sense that

$$(\forall i)(\exists c)[KS_i[g(n), S(n)] \subseteq KS_u[g(n) + c, cS(n)]] \ .$$

Theorem 8 (Invariance Theorem, time bounded variant [Har83]).
There is a Turing machine M_u which is nearly optimal, in the sense that

$$(\forall i)(\exists c)[KT_i[g(n), T(n)] \subseteq KT_u[g(n) + c, cT(n) \log T(n)]] \ .$$

In other words, any string that has a short description with respect to M_i has also a short description with respect to M_u. This means that we can safely omit the index, implicitly referring to a fixed chosen optimal Turing machine M_u. All the theorems derived later are unaffected by the additive constant factor in the description length, and by the multiplicative factor in the resource bounds.

We also need to define conditional Kolmogorov complexity. Intuitively, this gives the size of the shortest description of a string x, where an integer m is available to recompute x from its description:

Definition 9. For a Turing machine M_i, a space bound $S(n)$ and a function $g(n) \geq 1$, and a value m the space bounded conditional Kolmogorov complexity set is defined as follows:

$$KS[g(n) \,|\, m, S(n)] = \{x \mid (\exists y)[|y| \leq g(|x|) \text{ and } M_u(\langle y, m \rangle) = x,$$
$$\text{using at most } S(|x|) \text{ space}\} \ .$$

The Invariance Theorems are also valid when using conditional complexity, so again we can omit the index in the notation. The value m in the above definition could be a function of x. In this paper, we will use conditional complexity $KS[g(n)\,|n, S(n)]$, where n is the size of x, to make abstraction of the length of the string to be printed. As the Kolmogorov complexity gives the shortest description of a string x, including its length, the conditional Kolmogorov complexity $K(x\,|\,|x|)$ makes abstraction of the length of the string to be printed (we do not need to code the length of x in the description).

3 Statistical Tests

Our aim is to show that the Kolmogorov random strings possess many statistical properties. Martin-Löf [ML66] gave a definition of statistical test, and showed that the Kolmogorov random strings possess all the computable properties of random strings. For example, while a binary string picked at random has a *high probability* of having about the same number of 0's and 1's, a Kolmogorov random string *will* have that property.

One might consider a test that classifies the strings as random or non-random. But Martin-Löf wanted to consider strings that have various levels of randomness. For example, it might be awkward to classify a string starting with 9 zeroes as random and a string starting with 10 zeroes as non-random. We would prefer to design a test that detects more and more non-randomness as the number of leading zeroes increases. With this in mind, a Martin-Löf statistical test will have many levels of significance to differentiate between non-random strings and highly non-random strings. The strings which have a high degree of non-randomness will fail the test at high levels. The number of strings that fail the test should decrease as the level increases. Martin-Löf considers exponential decrease. It is understood that a test is checking only a specific property of the strings, and some K-non-random strings could easily be called totally random by a specific test.

It is also inherent in a test that very few strings are considered non-random, and that most strings are considered random (a test classifies a string as non-random if it has some characteristic not shared by most of the strings).

A *level* of a statistical test is a set of strings which the test finds relatively non-random. Each level is a subset of the previous level, containing fewer and fewer strings, considered more and more non-random. So, we can consider that a statistical test measures the *non-randomness* of a string.

It is required that the number of strings decrease exponentially fast at each level. If we take a specific test, the level 0 contains all the strings, the level 1 at most $1/2$ of the strings, the level 2 at most $1/4$ of the strings, and so on. This counting should be valid for any fixed n, if we consider only the set of strings of length n. The level m thus contains at most 2^{n-m} strings of length n.

Definition 10. A test F is a set of pairs $\langle m, s \rangle$, m integer and $s \in \{0, 1\}^*$, such that

1. $(\forall x)[\langle 0, x \rangle \in F]$
2. $(\forall x)(\forall m \geq 1)[\langle m, x \rangle \in F \Rightarrow \langle m - 1, x \rangle \in F]$
3. $(\forall m)(\forall n)[\#\{\langle m, x \rangle \,|\, \langle m, x \rangle \in F \text{ and } |x| = n\} \leq 2^{n-m}]$.

The first condition insures that all strings are considered non-random at level 0. The second condition insures that there is only one level at which a string becomes random. The third condition forces the density of the non-random strings to decrease with the level.

We define the level of x with respect to the test F as the maximum level at which x is considered non-random:

$$m_F(x) = \max\{m \mid \langle m, x \rangle \in F\} \ .$$

So, a test can be defined either as a set F, or as a function m_F.

We should note that according to the definition, any test F assigns to each string x a level of at most $|x|$: $0 \leq m_F(x) \leq |x|$. The string x is considered non random if $m_F(x)$ is close to $|x|$.

From the definition, it is possible to have a test F for which $m_F(x) = 0$ for each x. This kind of test does not detect any non randomness. We will later need a test detecting the maximum possible number of strings allowed by the definition of statistical test.

Definition 11. A *full range* test is a test having exactly 2^{n-m} strings of length n at level m.

An example of a full range test is a test classifying strings according to how many leading zeroes the string has.

We will be able to show that if a statistical test does not take too much space, then it never gives a high level to a SBK-random string. In fact, the level assigned to a SBK-random string is bounded by a constant. Proving this will be equivalent to proving that the set $\overline{KS[n - 1, S(n)]}$ *passes* space bounded tests.

Definition 12. The set A *passes* the test $F \Leftrightarrow$

$$(\exists c)(\forall x)[x \in A \Rightarrow m_F(x) \leq |x| - \log(|\overline{A_{|x|}}|) + c] \ .$$

where the notation A_n means the set of all strings of A of size n.

This definition says that a set passes a test if all the elements of the set are in the lowest level possible (allowing a constant number of levels more). This is significant when the set does not contain almost all the strings. Note that Σ^* passes any test. If the set contains at most a fixed fraction α of the strings, then *passing a test* means that all the elements are contained in the lowest c levels, for some constant c. If the set A is empty, it passes the test. However, finite non-empty sets could fail to pass a test. Also note that if F is a full range test, and both the set A and $\overline{A}$ contain more than a constant number of strings of each length, then either A or $\overline{A}$ will not pass the test.

4 Random Strings and Statistical Tests

Martin-Löf [ML66] proved that the K-random strings possess all the computable statistical properties. Here by computable, we really mean that the set F is recursively enumerable. He proved this by first constructing a *universal* test, which is optimal up to a constant factor. This means that a string passing the universal test at level l will pass any other computable test at a level within a constant of l. Then, he proved that any K-random string pass this universal test, concluding that it will pass every computable test.

In this section we offer a proof of his theorem. This proof will be used in later sections. Although our proof below is based on the same idea, we take a different approach. The basic idea in our proof of his theorem is that if according to some test, a string has a high level, the string has a short description, due to the fact that the level is limited in size. Because of this, the string could not be K-random. We can in fact say more. The maximum level a string can reach according to a test provides an upper bound on the K-complexity of the string. So, our proof doesn't need the universal test. Moreover, the universal test can easily be constructed once the theorem has been proven.

The universal test turns out to be very important in our understanding of the subject. Indeed, while K-complexity measures in which proportion the string is random, the universal test measures in which proportion the string is non-random, and these two measures will always add up to the length of the string (up to a constant factor).

Theorem 13. *For any function $g(n) \geq 0$, the set $\overline{K[g(n)\,|n]}$ passes any computable (r.e.) test F.*

Proof. Let F be a computable (r.e.) test, and let M_i be a machine accepting F. Let $A = \overline{K[g(n)\,|n]}$.

The set $\overline{A} = K[g(n)\,|n]$ has at least $2^{g(n)-k}$ strings of size n, for some k because any string that has $n - g(n) + k$ leading zeroes can be printed efficiently by a program of size $g(n)$, if k is chosen appropriately.

The set $\overline{A}$ has at most $2^{g(n)}$ strings of size n, because there are at most this many programs of size $g(n)$. This means that

$$g(n) - k \leq \log(|\overline{A_{|x|}}|) \leq g(n) \ .$$

To show that A passes the test F, we have to show that

$$(\exists c)(\forall x)\,[x \notin K[g(n)\,|n] \Rightarrow m_F(x) \leq n - g(n) + c] \ . \tag{1}$$

We show that

$$(\exists c)(\forall x)\,[x \in K[n - m_F(x) + c\,|n]] \ . \tag{2}$$

Notice that if $m_F(x) > |x| - g(|x|) + c$, then

$$x \in K[n - m_F(x) + c\,|n] \Rightarrow x \in K[n - (n - g(n) + c) + c\,|n] = K[g(n)\,|n] \ .$$

So, from (2) we can get that

$$(\exists c)(\forall x)\left[m_F(x) > |x| - g(|x|) + c \Rightarrow x \in K[g(n)\,|n]\right] . \tag{3}$$

which is equivalent to (1).

To show (2), we need to construct a program reconstructing x from a description of appropriate length.

Let A be the set of all strings of level $m_F(x)$:

$$A = \{x'|m_F(x') = m_F(x) \text{ and } |x'| = |x|\}$$

We can say, from the definition of a test, that $|A| \leq 2^{|x|-m_F(x)}$.

Let i be the canonical order of x in A. From a binary expansion of i of length exactly $|x| - m_F(x)$ and an algorithm for F, and also given $|x|$, we can compute x. We first compute $m_F(x) = |x| - |i|$. We then enumerate A, which is the level m of F, and print the ith element of A.

The length of the program is $|x| - m_F(x) + c$ for some constant c. We can conclude that $x \in K[n - m_F(x) + c\,|n]$. $\qquad\square$

Notice that we did not need that $g(n)$ be computable in the previous proof. Also, we didn't have any upper bound on $g(n)$. However, if $g(n) > n$, then the theorem becomes trivially true, because of our definition of passing a test.

To prove the theorem, Martin-Löf first built a universal test by simulating all computable tests at once, and then showed that the level given by this test to a string x is $|x| - g(|x|) + c$. This universal test is very important in understanding the properties of random sequences. ¿From Theorem 13, we can easily build a universal test.

Theorem 14. *There is a r.e. test F such that for any r.e. test T, $(\exists c)\,[m_F(x) \geq m_T(x) - c]$.*

Proof. Let F be the test defined as follows.

$$\langle m, x\rangle \in F \Leftrightarrow K(x\,|\,n) + m \leq |x| .$$

To see if $\langle m, x\rangle \in F$, simulate (using dovetailing) all programs of size $|x| - m$. If one of them halts and prints x, then accept x. This means that F is r.e.

From the definition of F, we know that $n - m_F(x) = K(x\,|n)$, so for any string x, $x \notin K[n - m_F(x) + 1\,|n]$. By Theorem 13, for any function g,

$$(\exists c)(\forall x)\left[x \notin K[g(n)\,|n] \Rightarrow m_T(x) \leq n - g(n) + c\right] .$$

Looking more carefully at the proof of Theorem 13, we notice that the constant c does not depend on the function g, so we can write

$$(\exists c)(\forall x)(\forall g)\left[x \notin K[g(n)\,|n] \Rightarrow m_T(x) \leq n - g(n) + c\right] .$$

Now, letting $g(n) = n - m_F(x) + 1$, we can conclude that:

$$(\exists c)(\forall x)m_T(x) \leq n - (n - m_F(x) + 1) + c ,$$

which means that

$$m_F(x) \geq m_T(x) - c .$$

$\qquad\square$

Let F_u denote the universal statistical test. The construction of the universal test above, and the fact that any universal test will give the same level to any string (within an additive constant factor) provides the following interesting corollary, that says that the Kolmogorov complexity and the level given by a universal test are complementary:

Corollary 15. *For any universal test F_u, there is a constant c such that for any string x,*

$$K(x\,|n) + m_{F_u}(x) = |x| \pm c \ .$$

5 The Space Bound Equivalent

In this section, we first show that the set of SBK-random strings passes any statistical test using less space. We further show how to design a test requiring just a little more space, and which the set of SBK-random strings does not pass. Since our theorems will be sensitive to multiplicative constants in the space bounds, we need to introduce a refinement of the standard space complexity.

Definition 16. $\mathrm{SPACE}_u[S(n)]$ is the class of sets accepted by a program running on the universal Turing machine M_u in space $S(n)$.

This definition is a refinement space complexity because

$$\mathrm{SPACE}[S(n)] = \cup_u \mathrm{SPACE}_u[S(n)] \ .$$

Also notice that the space compression theorem does not apply in this space complexity, so it is important to keep constant factors.

Theorem 17. *Let $S(n) > n$ and $g(n)$ be any function on natural numbers. Let F be a test such that $m_F(x)$ can be computed in $SPACE_u[S(|x|) - 4|x|]$. Then $\overline{KS[g(n)\,|n, S(n)]}$ passes the test F.*

Proof. We have to modify the proof of Theorem 13 to account for space bounds. In Theorem 13, we show how to construct x from a description of size $n - m_F(x) + c$. Let's look at how much space is involved in constructing x from its description. We need to enumerate the set A. To do that, we need to simulate F on every string of the same size as x. The space needed is the space used by F, $S(n) - 4n$, space n to keep the current input being tried, space n to keep the current output, space n to keep the target index, space n to keep the current index, for a total of at most $S(n)$. $\square$

Now, we show that if we have a little more space, the situation is reversed.

Theorem 18. *For any $S(n) > n$ space constructible on M_u, there is a full range test F in $SPACE_u[2S(n) + O(n)]$ which detects $\overline{KS[g(n)\,|n, S(n)]}$, in the sense that $m_F(x) \neq 0 \Rightarrow x \notin KS[g(n)\,|n, S(n)]$, for any $g(n) < n - 1$.*

Proof. The idea is to put only strings that are somewhat random at every non-zero level of the test F. First, F contains all the pairs $\langle 0, x \rangle$. For $m > 0$, let $A_{n,m}$ be the first 2^{n-m} elements of $\overline{KS[n-2\,|n, S(n)]}$ of length n in a canonical enumeration of that set. Then, $\langle m, x \rangle \in F \Leftrightarrow x \in A_{|x|,m}$.

The test F is a full range test, because the set $\overline{KS[n-2\,|n, S(n)]}$ has at least 2^{n-1} strings of length n, so F contains exactly 2^{n-m} strings of length n at level m.

Now, if $m_F(x) \neq 0$, then $x \notin KS[g(n)\,|n, S(n)]$ because each string of the set is given the highest possible level, with the constraint that the number of strings at each level is limited. Because $\overline{KS[n-2\,|n, S(n)]}$ contains at least half of the strings of length n, its strings fill up all the levels but level 0.

Since $\overline{KS[n-2\,|n, S(n)]} \subset \overline{KS[g(n)\,|n, S(n)]}$, we can deduce that F detects $KS[g(n)\,|n, S(n)]$, for any $g(n)$.

It remains to show that the test F can be computed within the claimed space bound. Given $\langle x, m \rangle$, compute $S(|x|)$ and mark off the space. Distribute the marks at every even position on each tape. This will allow us to do the simulation of programs on the odd positions while making sure the program does not exceed its space bound. Then start enumerating $\overline{KS[n-1\,|n, S(n)]}$ by simulating in order all the programs of size $\leq n-1$. While doing the simulation, we check that the program does not exceed space $S(n)$. We also need to check that the program does not loop. To do this, we need to count the steps of the simulated program. If the program runs for more than $2^{S(n)}$ steps without exceeding its space bound, then we know that it will never halt. Without loss of generality, we can assume that M_u has an alphabet large enough that we can combine the marks with the counter on the even positions of the tape. In addition to the space required for the simulation, we need to remember the program being simulated and an index for the stage of the enumeration. All of this can be stored in $O(n)$ space. $\qquad\square$

In fact, this technique can be used to find a test in $\mathrm{SPACE}_u[2S(n) + O(n)]$ to detect any set A in $\mathrm{SPACE}_u[S(n)]$.

Next, we address the question of the space bounded universal test. We can construct a universal test, which detects anything that can be detected by a test in $\mathrm{SPACE}_u[S(n)]$.

Theorem 19. *If $S(n)$ is space constructible on M_u, then there is a test F in $SPACE_u[2S(n) + O(n)]$ such that for any test T in $SPACE_u[S(n)]$,*

$$(\exists c)\,[m_T(x) = f(|x|) \Rightarrow m_F(x) \geq f(|x|) - c]\ .$$

Proof. For each Turing machine M_i, let $M_i{}'$ be the machine which accepts x if and only if M_i accepts x without using more than $S(n)$ space. Using the simulation described in Theorem 18, $M_i{}'$ uses $2S(n)$. The test F_i is defined as follows. All the pairs $\langle 0, x \rangle$ are in F_i. For $m > 0$, $\langle m, x \rangle$ is in $F_i \Leftrightarrow [\,x \in L(M_i{}')$ and there are at most 2^{n-m} strings y of length n smaller than x such that $y \in L(M_i{}')\,]$. Using the simulation above and $O(n)$ space for indices, we have that F_i is in $\mathrm{SPACE}_u[2S(n) + O(n)]$.

Now, every test in $\text{SPACE}_u[S(n)]$ is an F_i for some i. The universal test F is defined in the following way:

$$\langle m, x \rangle \in F \Leftrightarrow (\exists 0 \leq k \leq |x| - m)\,[\langle m + k, x \rangle \in F_k]\ .$$

The test F uses an additional n space to store an index for k, so $F \in \text{SPACE}_u[2S(n) + O(n)]$. The test is universal because

$$m_{F_i}(x) = f(|x|) \Rightarrow m_F(x) \geq f(|x|) - i\ .$$

$\square$

6 The Time Bound Equivalent

The same techniques as in section 5 can be applied to the time bounded Kolmogorov classes. However, the results here are much looser, mainly because time is not a reusable resource. It requires $2^n T(n)$ time bound to insure that a Kolmogorov random string passes the $T(n)$ bounded tests, and vice-versa. We first need to define the finer notion of time complexity, as we did for time.

Definition 20. $\text{TIME}_u[T(n)]$ is the class of sets accepted by a program running on the universal Turing machine M_u in time $T(n)$.

Theorem 21. *There is a constant c such the the following holds. Let $T(n) > n^2$ and $g(n)$ be any function on natural numbers. Let F be a test such that $m_F(x)$ can be computed in $TIME_u[T(|x| - c|x|^2 + |x|]$. Then $\overline{KT[g(n)\,|n, 2^n T(n)]}$ passes the test F.*

Proof. Same as in the proof of Theorem 17, but calculating the time requirements instead.

$\square$

Theorem 22. *There is a constant c such that for any $T(n) > n^2$ computable on M_u in time $T(n)$, there is a full range test F in $TIME_u[c2^n T(|x|)+cn^2]$ which detects $\overline{KT[g(n)\,|n, T(n)]}$, in the sense that $m_F(x) \neq 0 \Rightarrow x \notin KT[g(n)\,|n, T(n)]$, for any $g(n) < n$.*

Proof. Same as in the proof of Theorem 18, but calculating the time requirements instead.

$\square$

We do not expect that the bound can be improved in the last two theorems. The problem seems to have a relation with the power of nondeterminism. Assuming $\text{NTIME}[T(n)] \subseteq \text{TIME}[T_2(n)]$, for some other reasonable time bound T_2, we can show that the $2^n T(n)$ time bound can be reduced to $cn2^{g(n)}T_2(n)$ in both theorems. If $g(n) \leq c\log(n)$ for some c, and if T_2 is not too large, then the exponential multiplicative factor has been reduced to polynomial.

Theorem 23. *Suppose $NTIME[T(n)] \subseteq TIME[T_2(n)]$. Then, the $2^n T(n)$ can be replaced by $n2^{g(n)}T_2(n)$ in Theorems 21 and 22. (In Theorem 22, we would also need that $g(n)$ is computable in time $T(n)$.)*

Proof. The time blow up in Theorems 21 and 22 is due to the enumeration of sets. If the membership in a set A can be computed in time $T(n)$, then the set

$$\{\langle n, x\rangle \mid (\exists y \in A) \text{ of length } n \text{ such that } x \text{ is a prefix of } y\}$$

is in NTIME$[T(n)]$. If this set can be computed in DTIME$[T_2]$, then one can enumerate the first i elements of A in time $cniT_2(n)$. $\qquad\square$

On the other hand, for each time constructible function $T(n)$, there is an oracle A under which a $2^{n-g(n)-c}$ factor is required to the relativized time bounded K-random strings to pass all the $T(n)$ time bounded tests. Again, if $g(n) \leq c\log(n)$ for some c, this is almost an exponential multiplicative factor.

Theorem 24. *Let $T(n)$ be time constructible on M_u. Then, there is an oracle A and a test T in $TIME^A[T(n)]$ and a constant c such that for any $g(n)$, $\overline{KT^A[g(n)\,|n, 2^{n-g(n)-c}T(n)]}$ does not pass T.*

Proof. For some specific values of n, we will put a string of length n at the higher level of T. The test T works as follows. A string x is either at level 0 or at level $|x|$. To determine if a string x is at level $|x|$, compute $T(|x|)$. Make a query of all extensions of x in increasing order of length to the oracle A. If any query is successful, put x at level $|x|$. If no query is successful when the time expires (after at least $\frac{T(n)}{2^{c_2}}$ queries, for some c_2), put x at level 0.

Now, we define A to insure that T is a test and that

$$S = \overline{KT^A[g(n)\,|n, 2^{n-g(n)-c}T(n)]}$$

does not pass T.

Let $c > c_2 + 1$. For our specific n, we look at the set of all strings queried by any program of length $g(n)$ during its computation of length $2^{n-g(n)-c}T(n)$, using for oracle the part of A that has been determined so far and answering no to any new query. There are at most $2^{n-c}T(n)$ of these strings. Take a string x of length n such that for some extension y of x of length at most $n + \log(T(n)/c_2)$, y has not been queried. Such a string exists because at least half of the strings x are available and if for all of them, all extensions have been queried, it means there would have been at least $2^{n-1-c_2}T(n) > 2^{n-c}T(n)$ queries. Put this string y in A. This ensures that x is at level $|x|$ and is in S.

We now need to do this for infinitely many n. To pick up a new n, we just need to be sure that not too many strings of similar size will be put in A, as that could put more than one string x at level $|x|$. To do that, we just need to choose $n_{i+1} > n_i + \log(T(n))$. $\qquad\square$

7 Random Number Generators

Random number generators have many applications for cryptographic protocols [BM84, VV83] and randomizing algorithms. One can think of a pseudo-random number generator as a deterministic process, which from a finite seed, produces an infinite sequence of bits that hopefully possess all the desirable statistical properties of a real random source. Such processes have been proposed and analyzed with respect to some statistical properties [Knu69], or with respect to predictors trying to detect their output [Wil83].

The second kind of pseudo-random number generator is the one that produces a finite long string from a short string obtained from a real random source. Yao [Yao82] gave a definition of a good polynomial-time pseudo-random number generator of this kind and many candidates have been suggested. Essentially, a pseudo-random number generator is good if it cannot be distinguished from a real random source by any efficient program.

We see that our tight relation on the space bounded case have direct consequences on space bounded random number generation. The following theorems are a direct simple application of the previous sections. They state that if a generator can use a little more space, it can produce random looking bits. On the other hand, if a test can use a little more space, then it can detect the non-randomness. (See also [Wil83] for a deeper analysis of generators and predictors not relying on Kolmogorov complexity and [Ko86] for a study of infinite strings in a polynomial time bound setting.)

Theorem 25. *There is a statistical test which can detect any random number generator bounded in space and starting from a finite seed, using just a little more space.*

Proof. Because the generator uses a finite seed, all the prefixes of its output string are in $KS[c\,|n, S(n)]$ for some constant c. But Theorem 18 says that some test will detect this set. Moreover, Theorem 19 says that some fixed universal test will detect the set as well. $\square$

Theorem 26. *Let $S(n) > n$ be a nondecreasing function computable in $O(S(n))$ space. Then, there is a pseudo-random number generator producing an infinite string α from a finite seed, using at most $O(S(2n))$ space to produce the first n bits of the string, and for which for any n, $KS(\alpha_n\,|n, S(n)) \geq n/4 - 2\log(n)$.*

Proof. The generator produces the stream of bits by batches. Suppose at stage i we have produced α_m. Then, we consider all strings x of length $2m$ with α_m as prefix. We take a string x such that $KS(x\,|n, S(n))$ is maximized. Then, we output an $m/2$ bits extension of α_m according to the $m/2$ bits following α_m in x. The last portion of x is ignored.

For computing any bit, we use at most $O(S(2n))$ bits for computing the space bounded K-complexity of strings of length at most $2n$.

It can be shown by induction on i that the string α_m produced at stage i is such that $KS(\alpha_m\,|m, S(4m/3)) \geq m/3$ and that all of its prefixes y are such that $KS(y\,|\,|y|, S(n)) \geq |y|/4 - 3\log(|y|)$. $\square$

For the second kind of pseudo-random number generator, a generator can be seen as a device which, given an input of length n, outputs a longer string, say of length n^2. It differs from a pure random number generator by the strings it can output. A pure random number generator can output each of the 2^{n^2} possible strings of length n^2 with equal probability whereas the pseudo-random number generator will output at most 2^n different strings of length n^2, and not necessarily with the same probability.

Definition 27. A (Yao) *test* is a program which receives a string as input and answers 0 or 1.

Definition 28. Let G be a pseudo-random number generator and T be a test. Let $Pr_G(n)$ be the probability that the test answers 1 when given a string of length n^2 with the probability distribution induced from G on inputs of length n. Let $Pr_R(n)$ be the probability that the test answers 1 when given a string of length n^2 with a uniform distribution. Then, G *passes* the test if for any c, $|Pr_G(n) - Pr_R(n)|$ is in $O(1/(n^c))$.

Definition 29. A pseudo-random number generator is *perfect* if it passes all polynomial-time bounded tests.

The first question that comes to mind is whether the set of strings output by a perfect generator, passes the Martin-Löf statistical tests. Another question is whether a generator that would produce only Kolmogorov random strings would be perfect. These questions are answered in the following theorems.

Theorem 30. *Let A be a set of strings containing at most a constant fraction α of the strings of length n, for any n. Then, if A passes the Martin-Löf statistical tests, a random number generator outputting only the strings in the set is not perfect.*

Proof. Let A be as stated in the theorem. One Martin-Löf statistical test would count the number of leading zeroes in a string. If A passes this test, the number of leading zeroes is bounded by a constant c. Now, let p be a program counting the number of leading zeroes and answering 1 if more than c zeroes have been found. For p, the probability of answering 1 given a string from A is exactly 0. However, given a random string, the probability is $2^{-(c+1)}$. This difference is enough to say that the generator is not perfect. $\qquad\square$

Corollary 31. *If a pseudo-random number generator is perfect, the set of strings output by the generator doesn't pass Martin-Löf's test.*

We now know that the definition of "passing a test" based on Martin-Löf's definition differs from Yao's definition [Yao82]. We can explain the difference as follows.

The reason a generator outputting only K-random strings is not suitable is that a real random number generator will sometimes output non-random strings. Even if this happens relatively infrequently, a polynomial time test can detect it with a probability which is sufficient to unqualify the pseudo-random source. Yao's definition is oriented to categorize the random number generators which, given a seed, output a longer finite random sequences. It analyzes the statistical properties of the set of strings output by the generator. Martin Löf's tests is designed to analyze the statistical properties of the pattern inside one long string.

So, maybe it would be better to make a generator output parts of a long K-random string instead of many K-random short strings. Indeed, we can have some relations between those two measures. In the following theorem, we look at the concatenation the strings output by a generator into a long string. The following theorem says that if we take a long K-random string, cut it into small strings and let the pseudo-random number generator G choose randomly among the few strings, then G is perfect.

Theorem 32. *Let G be a pseudo-random number generator. Let x_m be the concatenation of all 2^m strings of length m^2 given by G when we vary the seed over all possible strings of length m. Let $f(n)$ be a function such that for all k, $f(n) > \log^k n$ almost everywhere. Then,*

$$(\forall m)[x_m \notin KT[n - \frac{n}{f(n)} \mid n, 2^{n^2}]] \Rightarrow G \text{ is perfect .}$$

Proof. Let T be a polynomial-time (Yao) test. Let p be the probability that T answers 1, given a random string of length m^2. For a string y of length $m^2 2^m$, let S_y be the number of parts of y of length m^2 for which T answers 1. If every bit of y is chosen randomly (by flipping a fair coin), S_y is a binomial random variable with probability p of success for each 2^m trial. The expected value of S_y is $2^m p$. For the test T to fail on a string z, T must answer 1 with probability that differs from p by at least $1/m^c$, for some c. This means that either $S_z \geq 2^m(p + 1/m^c)$ or that $S_z \leq 2^m(p - 1/m^c)$. Let A_m be the set of strings z of length $m^2 2^m$ such that T fails on z. If z is chosen randomly, an upper bound on the probability that $z \in A_m$ is calculated using the Chernoff bounds [Che52]. We will use the following simply stated bounds (see [AV79]):

For a binomial distribution with n experiments and for $0 < \epsilon < 1$

$$\text{Prob}[S_n \leq \lfloor (1 - \epsilon)np \rfloor] \leq e^{-\epsilon^2 np/2}$$

$$\text{Prob}[S_n \geq \lceil (1 + \epsilon)np \rceil] \leq e^{-\epsilon^2 np/3} .$$

For our case, using $n = 2^m$ and $\epsilon = 1/mp^c$, this means that

$$\text{Prob}[z \in A_m] \leq e^{- \frac{1}{p^2 m^{2c}} 2^m p/3} + e^{- \frac{1}{p^2 m^{2c}} 2^m p/2} \leq 2^{- \frac{b2^m}{pm^{2c}}} ,$$

for some constant b.

Since there are $2^{m^2 2^m}$ strings of length $m^2 2^m$, an upper bound on the number of strings in A_m is:

$$|A_m| \leq 2^{m^2 2^m - \frac{b2^m}{pm^{2c}}} .$$

This means that those strings can be described by their index of size $m^2 2^m - \frac{b2^m}{pm^{2c}}$. If $n = m^2 2^m$, then the description size is at most $n - \frac{n}{\log^k n}$, for some k that depends on c, or at most $n - n/f(n)$.

To compute x_m from its description, first compute p by simulating T on all strings of length m^2. Then, simulate T using all possible strings y of length

$m^2 2^m$ computing S_y. Knowing S_y will tell if $y \in A_m$. Stop the simulation when the right index has been reached. This takes time at most 2^{n^2}.

We can conclude that if G is not perfect, then the string x_m is in $KT[n - \frac{n}{f(n)} \,|\, n, 2^{n^2}]]$. $\qquad\qquad\qquad\qquad\qquad\qquad\qquad\qquad\qquad\qquad\qquad\qquad\square$

This last theorem is intended as showing a relation between Martin-Löf's statistical tests. It gives a sufficient condition based on space bounded Kolmogorov complexity for the existence of a secure pseudo random number generator. The above construction cannot be used in practice, because the generator constructed requires double exponential time. This brings an interesting problem. What is a sufficient condition (perhaps based on time bounded Kolmogorov complexity) that enables us to build an efficient pseudo random number generator?

References

[AV79]   D. Angluin and L.G. Valiant. Fast probabilistic algorithms for hamiltonian paths and matchings. *Comp. Syst. Sci.*, 18:155–193, 1979.

[BM84]   M. Blum and S. Micali. How to generate cryptographically strong sequences of pseudo-random bits. *SIAM J. Comput.*, 13:850–864, 1984.

[Cha69]   G. Chaitin. On the length of programs for computing finite binary sequences: statistical considerations. *J. Assoc. Comput. Mach.*, 16:145–159, 1969.

[Che52]   H. Chernoff. A measure of asymptotic efficiency for tests of hypothesis based on the sum of observations. *Annals of Math. Statistics*, 23, 1952.

[Chu40]   A. Church. On the concept of a random sequence. *Bulletin of the American Mathematical Society*, 46:130–135, 1940.

[Fin73]   T. Fine. *Theories of Probability*. Academic Press, 111 Fifth Avenue, New York, NY 10003, 1973.

[Har83]   J. Hartmanis. Generalized Kolmogorov complexity and the structure of feasible computations. In *Proc. 24th IEEE Symposium on Foundations of Computer Science*, pages 439–445, 1983.

[Knu69]   D. Knuth. *SemiNumerical Algorithms*, volume 2 of *The Art of Computer Programming*. Addison-Wesley, Reading, MA, 1969.

[Ko86]   K. Ko. On the notion of infinite pseudorandom sequences. *Theoretical Computer Science*, 48:9–13, 1986.

[Kol33]   A. Kolmogorov. *Grundbegriffe der Wahrscheinlichkeitsrechnung*. Springer Verlag, Berlin, 1933.

[Kol56]   A. Kolmogorov. *Foundations of the Theory of Probability*. Chelsea, Bronx, New York, 1956. Translation by N. Morrison.

[Kol63]   A. Kolmogorov. On tables of random numbers. *Sankhyi, The Indian Journal of Statistics, Series A*, 25:369–376, 1963.

[Kol65]   A. Kolmogorov. Three approaches for defining the concept of information quantity. *Prob. Inform. Trans.*, 1:1–7, 1965.

[Lon86]   L. Longpré. *Resource bounded Kolmogorov complexity, a link between computational complexity and information theory*. PhD thesis, Cornell University, 1986. Technical Report TR86-776.

[LV88]   M. Li and P.M.B. Vitányi. Two decades of applied kolmogorov complexity. In *Proc. Structure in Complexity Theory third annual conference*, pages 80–101, 1988.

[LV91]   M. Li and P.M.B. Vitányi. An introduction to kolmogorov complexity and its applications, part 1: Theory. Technical Report Note CS-R9101, Centrum voor Wiskunde en Informatica, P.O. Box 4079, 1009 AB Amsterdam, The Netherlands, 1991. Preliminary version of a textbook.

[ML66]   P. Martin-Löf. The definition of random sequences. *Information and Control*, 9:602–619, 1966.

[Sip83]   M. Sipser. A complexity theoretic approach to randomness. In *Proc. 15th ACM Symposium on Theory of Computing*, pages 330–335, 1983.

[Sol64]   R. Solomonoff. A formal theory of inductive inference, part 1 and part 2. *Information and Control*, 7:1–22, 224–254, 1964.

[Vil39]   J. Ville. *Etude critique de la notion de collectif.* Gauthier-Villars, Paris, 1939.

[vL87]   M. van Lambalgen. Von Mises' definition of random sequences reconsidered. *Journal of Symbolic Logic*, 52(3):725–755, Sept. 1987.

[vM19]   R. von Mises. Grundlagen der wahrscheinlichkeitsrechnung. *Mathemat. Zeitsch.*, 5:52–99, 1919.

[vM39]   R. von Mises. *Probability, Statistics and Truth.* MacMillan, New York, 1939. Reprint: Dover, 1981.

[vMG64]   R. von Mises and H. Geiringer. *The Mathematical Theory of Probability and Statistics.* Academic Press, New York, 1964.

[VV83]   U. Vazirani and V. Vazirani. Trapdoor pseudo-random number generators with applications to protocol design. In *Proc. 24th IEEE Symp. on Foundations of Computer Science*, pages 23–30, 1983.

[Wal38]   A. Wald. Die Widerspruchsfreiheit des Kollektivbegriffs in der Wahrscheinlichkeitsrechnung. *Ergebnisse eines Mathematischen Kolloquiums*, 8:38–72, 1938.

[Wil83]   R. Wilber. Randomness and the density of hard problems. In *Proc. 24th IEEE Symp. on Foundations of Computer Science*, pages 335–342, 1983.

[Yao82]   A. Yao. Theory and applications of trapdoor functions. In *Proc. 23rd IEEE Symposium on Foundations of Computer Science*, pages 80–91, 1982.

Complexity and Entropy:
An Introduction to
the Theory of Kolmogorov Complexity *

Vladimir A. Uspensky

Department of Mathematical Logic
Faculty of Mechanics and Mathematics
Moscow Lomonosov University
V-234 Moscow, GSP-3, 119899 Russia
uspensky@globlab.msk.su

Contents.

1 Complexity, Entropy, and Randomness

Things can be large or small, and their size (the length or the volume or the
weight or so on) can be measured by a number. Besides, things can be simple
or complex, and their complexity can also be measured by a number. I do not
know to whom we are indebted for measuring sizes by numbers. It was Andrei
Kolmogorov [Kol65] who proposed to measure the complexity of a thing by a
natural number (i.e., a non-negative integer), and he developed the rudiments
of the theory.

Complexity of things (as opposed to the complexity of processes, e.g., of
computational processes) took the name *descriptional complexity*, or *Kolmogorov
complexity*. As will be seen here, in appropriate cases one may say "entropy"
instead of "complexity".

---

* Preparation of this paper was supported in part by the Institute of New Technologies
  at Moscow.

Thus we assume that there is a set Y of things, or objects, y's, and a total function "complexity of y" defined on Y. That function will be denoted by Compl and its possible values are $0, 1, 2, 3, ..., n, ..., \infty$. So the function Compl is a total function from Y to $\mathrm{I\!N} \cup \{\infty\}$. We do not put any further restrictions on Compl, but take it on an intuitive level as a measure of complexity, or a complexity function, or, shorter, a complexity.

Let Compl_1 and Compl_2 be two measures of complexity. Let us say that Compl_1 is *not worse* than Compl_2 if

$$\mathrm{Compl}_1(y) \underset{+}{\leq} \mathrm{Compl}_2(y).$$

Explanation. The notation $A(y) \underset{+}{\leq} B(y)$ means that for some constant c not depending on y and for all y, $A(y) \leq B(y) + c$ holds.

Let $\mathcal{Z}$ be some class of complexities, or (that is the same) of measures of complexity. Let Compl_0, belonging to $\mathcal{Z}$, be not worse than any complexity belonging to $\mathcal{Z}$. Then Compl_0 is called *optimal* in the class $\mathcal{Z}$. So a way of measuring complexity is called optimal if it gives, roughly speaking, the shortest complexities of things. Of course, a class of complexities may have no optimal one.

Any optimal complexity is called an *entropy*. It is possible that a class $\mathcal{Z}$ has several entropies, but any two entropies, Ent_1 and Ent_2, fulfill the following condition:

$$\mathrm{Ent}_1(y) \underset{+}{=} \mathrm{Ent}_2(y)$$

Explanation. The notation $A(y) \underset{+}{=} B(y)$ means that $|A(y) - B(y)| \underset{+}{\leq} 0$, or $A(y) \underset{+}{\leq} B(y) \ and \ B(y) \underset{+}{\leq} A(y)$.

Important Remark. There is no semantic problem when one speaks about *an* entropy related to some class of complexities. But in the theory of Kolmogorov complexity it is usual to speak about *the* entropy and even to denote it by a special notation. What does it mean? Here we have an *abus de langage* (after N.Bourbaki). Speaking about *the* entropy related to some class, one speaks in fact about *an arbitrary* entropy of that class. And the notation denotes any of such entropies. Of course, our statements must be invariant and do not change their truth value when a particular entropy changes to another one but still belonging to the same class. But we must be cautious. Let $\mathcal{V}$ and $\mathcal{W}$ be two classes of complexity functions, and let K be *the* entropy related to $\mathcal{V}$ and L be *the* entropy related to $\mathcal{W}$. In fact, K and L denote two families of entropies, or, it is better to say, any entropies of those two families. When we write $K(y) \underset{+}{\leq} L(y)$, we suppose that this relation $\underset{+}{\leq}$ holds for any particular entropy denoted by K and any particular entropy denoted by L (so there is an additive constant hidden in this relation depending on the choices of particular representatives of K and

L). But when we declare that K and L coincide (are *the same* entropy), we do not want to express the opinion that any entropy denoted by K coincides with any entropy denoted by L. That is, we understand the coincidence statement in the following way: for any of the entropies K and any of the entropies L, there exists a constant c such that $|K(y) - L(y)| < c$ for all y.

Terminological Remark. In literature on Kolmogorov complexity, the term "complexity" (synonymous with "complexity function" and "measure of complexity") is most often used in the sense of the term "entropy". But we make the distinction between those two terms: entropy is an optimal complexity.

As has already been said, there may be no entropy among complexity functions belonging to a class $\mathcal{Z}$. An important property of a class $\mathcal{Z}$ is that of having an entropy. In such case, we say that the *Solomonoff–Kolmogorov Theorem* holds for $\mathcal{Z}$.

There exist several important classes of complexities that contain entropies. And among those entropies, there are ones of special interest — namely, those entropies that can be used for a definition of randomness. Kolmogorov has proposed the following definition of randomness for an infinite binary sequence $a_1 a_2 a_3 \cdots a_n \cdots$: the sequence is called *random*, or, more exactly, *Kolmogorov random*, if

$$\mathrm{Ent}(a_1 \cdots a_n) \underset{+}{\geq} n,$$

where Ent is an entropy. Of course, the choice of Ent is to be specified. Not every sort of entropy goes to a "good" definition of randomness; a definition by Kolmogorov scheme is regarded as "good" if the class of Kolmogorov random sequences sprung up by that definition coincides with the class of sequences that are random in the sense of Martin-Löf (or are *typical sequences*; see [KU87a] and [KU87b] and [Mar66]).

To sum up: in order to define an entropy, one must define an appropriate class of complexities and show that the Solomonoff–Kolmogorov Theorem holds for that class.

1.1 Generation of Complexities by Means of an Encoding Procedure

The idea (due to Kolmogorov) is very simple. There are objects and there are descriptions (encodings) of objects, and the complexity of an object is the minimal size of its description.

In more detail, there is a set Y of objects y, and a set X of descriptions (names, encodings) x. There is a volume function ℓ defined on X; that ℓ is a function from X to $\mathbb{N}$. A *mode of description*, or a *description mode*, is an arbitrary set $E \subseteq X \times Y$. If $\langle x, y \rangle \in E$, then x is called a *description* (a *name*, an *encoding*) *of y with respect to E.* Thus an object y may have many descriptions and a description may serve as a description for many objects.

The *complexity of y with respect to* a description mode E is defined as follows:

$$\mathrm{Compl}_E(y) = \min\{\ell(x) : \langle x, y \rangle \in E\}.$$

We make the convention that $\mathrm{Compl}_E(y) = \infty$ if there is no x such that $\langle x, y \rangle \in E$.

Let $\mathcal{E}$ be a class of modes of description. Each mode $E \in \mathcal{E}$ gives the corresponding complexity function Compl_E. Then there arises the class $\mathcal{Z} = \mathcal{Z}(\mathcal{E})$ of all complexity functions related to the modes of $\mathcal{E}$, and one may ask whether the class $\mathcal{Z}$ contains an optimal function, or an entropy. If such an optimal function exists, then it corresponds to some description mode which is also called *optimal*.

Until now we have not imposed any restrictions on X, Y, E. It is reasonable to assume that X and Y consist of *constructive objects*, and E is a *generable* set (in the sense of Post) and, consequently, is a recursively *enumerable* set.

In the following exposition we shall restrict ourselves with the following simple case: Both X and Y are $\varXi$, where $\varXi$ is the set of all binary words, or finite binary sequences. The volume function ℓ is defined to be $\ell(\xi) = |\xi|$ for every $\xi \in \varXi$, where $|\xi|$ is the length of ξ.

1.2 Two Symmetric Relations and Four Entropies

Our task is to define—in a reasonable way—a class $\mathcal{E}$ of modes of description as a class of subsets of $\varXi \times \varXi$. Having this goal in mind, we define a binary relation on $\varXi$ which we shall call *the concordance relation*: u_1 and u_2 are called *concordant* if they have a mutual continuation, i.e., if there are $t_1, t_2 \in \varXi$ such that $u_1 t_1 = u_2 t_2$. This concordance relation will be denoted by γ.

Thus we have two natural binary relations on $\varXi$: the equality $=$ and the concordance γ. Both are symmetric and decidable (see Explanation in Sect.1.3).

Let α and β be two binary relation on $\varXi$. We say that a mode of description $E \subseteq \varXi \times \varXi$ *fulfills the* (α, β)-*property* if for every $x_1, x_2, y_1, y_2 \in \varXi$,

$$\langle x_1, y_1 \rangle \in E \wedge \langle x_2, y_2 \rangle \in E \wedge x_1 \alpha x_2 \;\Rightarrow\; y_1 \beta y_2.$$

Let us consider the class $\mathcal{E} = \mathcal{E}(\alpha, \beta)$ of all recursively enumerable modes of description that fulfill (α, β)-property and the related class $\mathcal{Z}^{\alpha,\beta} = \mathcal{Z}(\mathcal{E})$ of complexity functions. If the class $\mathcal{Z}^{\alpha,\beta}$ contains an optimal complexity function, that complexity function will be called (α, β)-*entropy*.

Now move from variable α and β to constants $=$ and γ. Taking $=$ or γ as α or β, we obtain four classes of complexity functions: $\mathcal{Z}^{=,=}$, $\mathcal{Z}^{=,\gamma}$, $\mathcal{Z}^{\gamma,=}$, $\mathcal{Z}^{\gamma,\gamma}$. For each of these four classes, the Solomonoff–Kolmogorov theorem is valid, so we have four entropies:

1. $(=, =)$-entropy, or $\mathbb{N}\mathbb{N}$-entropy,
2. $(=, \gamma)$-entropy, or $\mathbb{N}\varXi$-entropy,
3. $(\gamma, =)$-entropy, or $\varXi\mathbb{N}$-entropy, and
4. (γ, γ)-entropy, or $\varXi\varXi$-entropy.

Note. The notations $\mathbb{I}\mathbb{N}\mathbb{I}\mathbb{N}$, etc., have the following origin. In [US81] and [US87], the notation "Ξ" had the following meaning: the set of all binary words being considered together with relation γ. In place of the set of all binary words with the relation $=$ on that set, the set $\mathbb{N}$ of all natural numbers with the relation $=$ and the volume function $l(x) = \lfloor \log_2(x+1) \rfloor$ was considered. This volume function is induced by the following 1-1 correspondence between $\mathbb{N}$ and Ξ: zero $\sim \Lambda$, one ~ 0, two ~ 1, three ~ 00, four ~ 01, five ~ 10, and so on.

1.3 Two Approximation Spaces and Four Entropies

There is another way to come to the four basic entropies of Sect.1.2.

Any set of constructive objects with a decidable partial ordering defined on that set will be called an *approximation space.*

Explanation. The term "decidable" means that there is an algorithm to decide for any x' and x'', whether $x' \leq x''$ or not.

On an intuitive level, the elements of an approximation space can be taken as informations, and $x' \leq x''$ means that the information x'' is a refinement of the information x' (and hence x'' is closer than x' to some limit value to which both x' and x'' serve as approximations).

To develop a more attractive theory of approximation spaces, especially with the intention to apply this theory to an advanced theory of Kolmogorov complexity, one needs to include some additional requirements into the definition of an approximation space. For our goals, however, it suffices to have a decidable partial ordering. Moreover, only two approximation spaces will be considered: the bunch $\mathbb{B}$ and the tree $\mathbf{T}$. Their definitions follow immediately.

- The *bunch* $\mathbb{B}$:   The set of objects is Ξ, and the partial ordering $\leq$ is $=$, i.e., $u \leq w$ iff $u = w$.
- The *tree* $\mathbf{T}$:   The set of objects is Ξ. The partial ordering $\leq$ is defined as follows: $u \leq w$ iff u is a prefix of w (and w is a continuation of u), i.e., $\exists v [\, uv = w \,]$.

Let X and Y be two approximation spaces. The spaces X and Y will be treated, respectively, as the space of descriptions (names, encodings) and as the space of the objects described (named, encoded). Our near goal is to define the class $\mathcal{E}$ of acceptable description modes $E \subseteq X \times Y$.

We impose on E the following three requirements:

1. if $\langle x, y \rangle \in E$ and $x' \geq x$, then $\langle x', y \rangle \in E$,
2. if $\langle x, y \rangle \in E$ and $y' \leq y$, then $\langle x, y' \rangle \in E$, and
3. if $\langle x, y_1 \rangle \in E$ and $\langle x, y_2 \rangle \in E$, then there exists a y that $\langle x, y \rangle \in E$, $y_1 \leq y$, and $y_2 \leq y$.

Hence, the only cause of the existence of two different objects having the same description is the execution of the first requirement.

A description mode is called *acceptable* if it is (recursively) enumerable and fulfills all the above requirements.

If one wishes to relate a complexity function with any description mode, one needs to introduce a volume function ℓ defined on X. Here we are interested in the cases $X = \mathbb{B}$ and $X = \mathbb{T}$ only. In both these cases, we put $\ell(x) = |x|$ where $|x|$ is the length of x.

Now let us fix approximation spaces X and Y, and let us consider the class of all acceptable description modes and the corresponding class of complexities. Let us ask whether the Solomonoff–Kolmogorov theorem holds for that class, and, if it does hold, then the related entropy will be called XY *entropy*.

It turns out that the Solomonoff–Kolmogorov theorem is valid for four cases when X and Y is respectively $\mathbb{B}$ or $\mathbb{T}$:

1. For $X = \mathbb{B}$ and $Y = \mathbb{B}$, we have $\mathbb{B}\mathbb{B}$-entropy,
2. For $X = \mathbb{B}$ and $Y = \mathbb{T}$, we have $\mathbb{B}\mathbb{T}$-entropy,
3. For $X = \mathbb{T}$ and $Y = \mathbb{B}$, we have $\mathbb{T}\mathbb{B}$-entropy, and
4. For $X = \mathbb{T}$ and $Y = \mathbb{T}$, we have $\mathbb{T}\mathbb{T}$-entropy.

It is easy to see that $\mathbb{B}\mathbb{B}$-, $\mathbb{B}\mathbb{T}$-, $\mathbb{T}\mathbb{B}$-, $\mathbb{T}\mathbb{T}$-entropy respectively coincides with $(=,=)$-, $(=,\gamma)$-, $(\gamma,=)$-, (γ,γ)-entropy of Sect.1.2. Speaking on the coincidence, take into account the Important Remark of Sect.1.

1.4 The Ordering of the Four Entropies

Now we have four entropies, and any two of them, A and B, do not coincide; which means that the assertion $A(y) \underset{\bigoplus}{=} B(y)$ is not valid. Let us write $A < B$ if $A(y) \underset{\bigoplus}{\leq} B(y)$ but not vice versa. Then there is a partial ordering on the set of four entropies. That ordering can be shown by the following picture; Fig.1.

The picture is directed from bottom to top. That is, it shows that

$$\mathbb{B}\mathbb{T} < \mathbb{B}\mathbb{B}, \quad \mathbb{B}\mathbb{T} < \mathbb{T}\mathbb{T}, \quad \mathbb{B}\mathbb{B} < \mathbb{T}\mathbb{B}, \quad \mathbb{T}\mathbb{T} < \mathbb{T}\mathbb{B},$$

and, of course,

$$\mathbb{B}\mathbb{T} < \mathbb{T}\mathbb{B}.$$

On the other hand,

$$\text{neither } \mathbb{B}\mathbb{B} < \mathbb{T}\mathbb{T} \text{ nor } \mathbb{T}\mathbb{T} < \mathbb{B}\mathbb{B}.$$

1.5 Encoding-Free Generation of Complexities and Entropies

It turns out that the four entropies of Sect.1.4 admit an encoding-free definition with no use of such terms as "descriptions", "names", or "encodings".

As before and always, an entropy is defined as an optimal complexity function for some class $\mathcal{Z}$ of complexity functions; and all members of $\mathcal{Z}$ are functions from Y to $\mathbb{N} \cup \{\infty\}$. So our goal is to describe appropriate classes $\mathcal{Z}$.

Having this goal in mind, let us introduce two conditions, $\mathbf{C}$ and Σ, which could be imposed on a function f: $Y \to \mathbb{N} \cup \{\infty\}$.

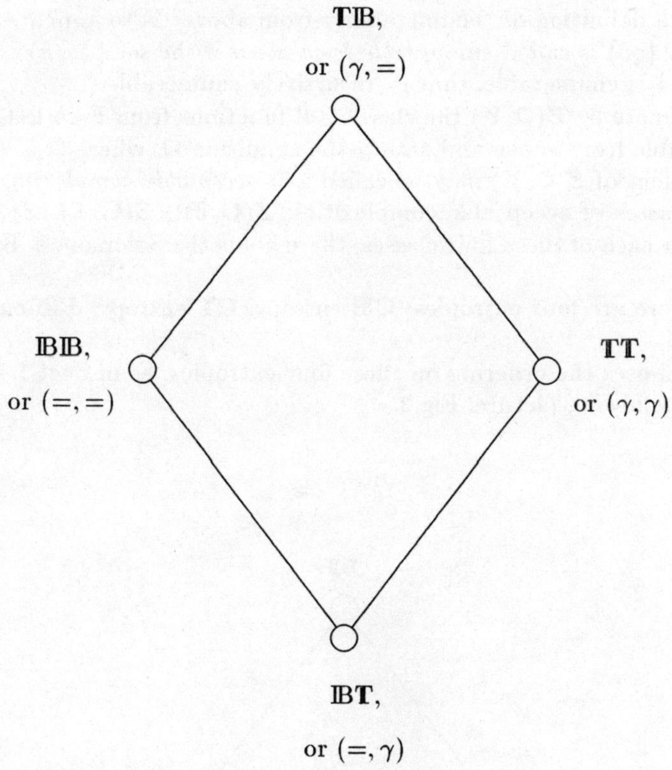

Fig. 1. The ordering of the four entropies: **TB**, **BB**, **TT**, **BT**

Condition C (of Cardinality of a set). Let $n \in \mathbf{N}$, and let $M \subseteq Y$ be an arbitrary set such that

1. any two elements of M are non-comparable, and
2. $M \subseteq f^{-1}(n)$.

Then the cardinality of M is less than or equal to 2^n.

Condition Σ (of summation of a series). Let $M \subseteq Y$ be an arbitrary set such that any two elements of M are non-comparable. Then

$$\sum_{y \in M} 2^{-f(y)} \leq 1.$$

Explanation. Elements y_1 and y_2 are *non-comparable* if neither $y_1 \leq y_2$ nor $y_2 \leq y_1$.

Thus, an arbitrary function f may or may not satisfy Condition **C** or Condition Σ. And it is easy to see that Condition Σ implies Condition **C**.

Further, a definition of "enumerability from above" is to appear. A function $f : Y \to \mathbb{N} \cup \{\infty\}$ is called *enumerable from above* if the set $\{\langle y, n \rangle : y \in Y, n \in \mathbb{N}, f(y) \leq n \}$ is enumerable, that is, recursively enumerable.

Let us denote by $\mathcal{Z}(\Box, Y)$ the class of all functions from Y to $\mathbb{N} \cup \{\infty\}$ that are enumerable from above and satisfy the condition $\Box$, where $\Box$ is either $\mathbf{C}$ or Σ. Any element of $\mathcal{Z}(\Box, Y)$ may be called a $\Box$-*acceptable complexity*. Hence, we have four classes of acceptable complexities: $\mathcal{Z}(\mathbf{C}, \mathbb{B})$, $\mathcal{Z}(\mathbf{C}, \mathbf{T})$, $\mathcal{Z}(\Sigma, \mathbb{B})$, and $\mathcal{Z}(\Sigma, \mathbf{T})$. For each of these four classes, there holds the Solomonoff–Kolmogorov theorem.

Thus, there are four entropies: $\mathbf{C}\mathbb{B}$-entropy, $\mathbf{C}\mathbf{T}$-entropy, $\Sigma\mathbb{B}$-entropy, and $\Sigma\mathbf{T}$-entropy.

If one imposes the ordering on these four entropies, as in Sect.1.4, then one obtains the following picture; Fig.2.

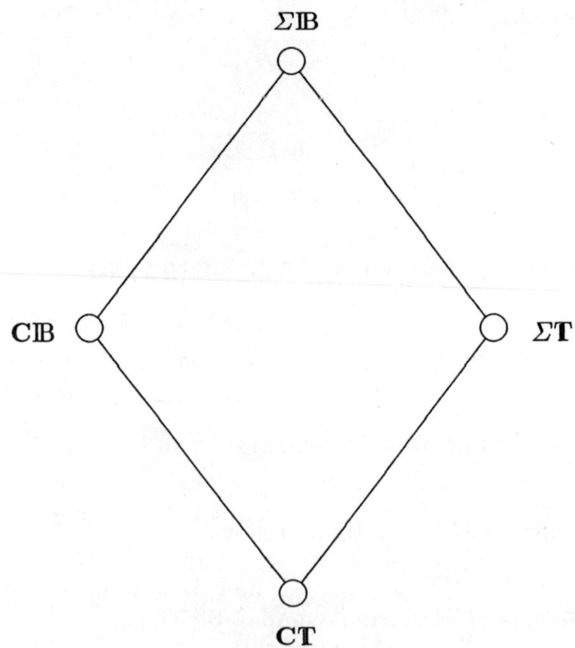

Fig. 2. The ordering of four entropies: $\Sigma\mathbb{B}$, $\mathbf{C}\mathbb{B}$, $\Sigma\mathbf{T}$, $\mathbf{C}\mathbf{T}$

The four entropies of this section also admit definitions with slightly modified versions of conditions $\mathbf{C}$ and Σ.

Condition $\mathbf{C'}$. There exists a constant b such that the cardinality of M is less than or equal to $b \cdot 2^n$ for every $M \subseteq Y$ satisfying the requirements (i) and (ii) of Condition **C**.

Condition Σ'. There exists a constant b such that

$$\sum_{y \in M} 2^{-f(y)} \leq b$$

for every $M \subseteq Y$ of mutually non-comparable elements.

Classes $\mathcal{Z}(\mathbf{C}', \mathbb{B})$, $\mathcal{Z}(\mathbf{C}', \mathbf{T})$, $\mathcal{Z}(\Sigma', \mathbb{B})$, and $\mathcal{Z}(\Sigma', \mathbf{T})$ differ from the corresponding classes $\mathcal{Z}(\mathbf{C}, \mathbb{B})$, $\mathcal{Z}(\mathbf{C}, \mathbf{T})$, $\mathcal{Z}(\Sigma, \mathbb{B})$, and $\mathcal{Z}(\Sigma, \mathbf{T})$; nevertheless, the related entropies coincide in the sense of Important Remark of Sect.1. That is,

$$\mathbf{C}'\mathbb{B} = \mathbf{C}\mathbb{B}, \ \ \mathbf{C}'\mathbf{T} = \mathbf{C}\mathbf{T}, \ \ \Sigma'\mathbb{B} = \Sigma\mathbb{B}, \ \ \text{and} \ \ \Sigma'\mathbf{T} = \Sigma\mathbf{T}.$$

Condition Σ^∞. For an arbitrary set $M \subseteq Y$ of mutually non-comparable elements,

$$\sum_{y \in M} 2^{-f(y)} < +\infty.$$

It is obvious that Condition Σ^∞ is equivalent to Condition Σ' for $Y = \mathbb{B}$. Hence, the $\Sigma^\infty\mathbb{B}$-entropy coincide with the $\Sigma'\mathbb{B}$-entropy and consequently with the $\Sigma\mathbb{B}$-entropy.

Theorem (Andrei Muchnik). *The conditions Σ' and Σ^∞ are equivalent in the case $Y = \mathbf{T}$.*

Hence the $\Sigma^\infty\mathbf{T}$-entropy coincides with the $\Sigma'\mathbf{T}$-entropy and with the $\Sigma\mathbf{T}$-entropy.

1.6 Relations between Two Quadruplets of Entropies

Now we have two quadruplets of entropies: the quadruplet $\mathbb{B}\mathbb{B}$, $\mathbb{B}\mathbf{T}$, $\mathbf{T}\mathbb{B}$, and $\mathbf{T}\mathbf{T}$, which respectively generated by means of encoding, and the quadruplet $\mathbf{C}\mathbb{B}$, $\mathbf{C}\mathbf{T}$, $\Sigma\mathbb{B}$, and $\Sigma\mathbf{T}$, which respectively generated by using some quantitative approach represented by conditions $\mathbf{C}$ and Σ.

It turns out that (in the sense of the equality explained in Sect.1, Important Remark) the following relations hold:

$$\mathbf{C}\mathbb{B} = \mathbb{B}\mathbb{B}, \ \ \mathbf{C}\mathbf{T} = \mathbb{B}\mathbf{T}, \ \ \text{and} \ \ \Sigma\mathbb{B} = \mathbf{T}\mathbb{B}.$$

As to $\Sigma\mathbf{T}$, we have the following non-trivial fact, which will be discussed in Sect.2.2(5):

$$\Sigma\mathbf{T} < \mathbf{T}\mathbf{T}.$$

Summarizing them, we obtain the following picture; Fig.3.

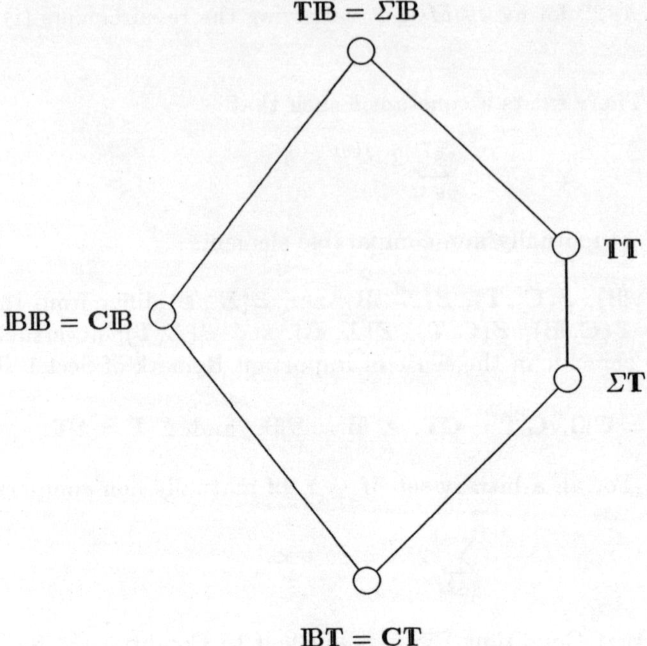

Fig. 3. The relation between entropies

1.7 A Semantic for $\Sigma\mathbf{T}$-Entropy

Four entropies of Fig.3 have an encoding semantic, but the fifth entropy, $\Sigma\mathbf{T}$, has not yet obtained an appropriate semantic. Now a semantic for $\Sigma\mathbf{T}$ will be set forth. That semantic is based upon probabilistic machines.

To this end let us consider a probabilistic Turing machine with one-way infinite output tape whose head moves in only one direction. "Probabilistic" means that one must flip a symmetric coin before performing any command, and the result of flipping determines which command is to be performed. Another version: at the input tape, there comes a random infinite binary sequence with equal probabilities of digits. We suppose that our machine has binary output alphabet and never stops, so a finite or infinite binary sequence appears on the output tape.

Let us fix a machine M. For any $y \in \Xi$, let us denote by $\mathrm{P}_M^n(y)$ the probability of the event 'y is the beginning of the output sequence'; in this notation, "n" stands for "non-stop". Consider a preorder relation $\leq$ on the set of machines: $M \leq N$ means that $\mathrm{P}_M^n(y) \underset{\cap}{\leq} \mathrm{P}_N^n(y)$.

Explanation. $A(y) \underset{\cap}{\leq} B(y)$ means that for some constant c not depending on y, and for every y, $A(y) \leq c \cdot B(y)$.

It turns out that there exists a *maximal* machine W such that $M \leq W$ for every machine M. In fact, there are several such machines, but any two of them, U and V, satisfy the condition

$$\mathrm{P}_U^n(y) \underset{\cap}{=} \mathrm{P}_V^n(y).$$

Explanation. $A(y) \underset{\cap}{=} B(y)$ iff $A(y) \underset{\cap}{\leq} B(y)$ and $B(y) \underset{\cap}{\leq} A(y)$.

Hence for any two maximal machines U and V, we have

$$\left|\log_2 \mathrm{P}_U^n(y)\right| \underset{\cap}{=} \left|\log_2 \mathrm{P}_V^n(y)\right|.$$

So we have moved from the probability P_W^n to its logarithm. For any maximal machine W one can verify that

$$\left|\log_2 \mathrm{P}_W^n(y)\right| \underset{\cap}{=} \Sigma\mathbf{T}(y)$$

This fact enables us to identify $\left|\log_2 \mathrm{P}_W^n\right|$ (or, if you prefer, the integer $\lfloor|\log_2 \mathrm{P}_W^n|\rfloor$) with $\Sigma\mathbf{T}$. (Recall again Important Remark of Sect.1). Then the probabilistic definition of P_W^n just given can be taken as a semantic for $\Sigma\mathbf{T}$.

The probability $\mathrm{P}_W^n(y)$, related to an arbitrary maximal machine W, can be called *a priori probability* of y as an element of the tree $\mathbf{T}$.

Remark. There exists also the a priori probability of y as an element of the bunch $\mathbb{B}$. To obtain the a priori probability of that second sort, one should consider probabilistic machines of a slightly different type. The change is: instead of machines that never stop, one should take now probabilistic machines that can stop. Then $\mathrm{P}_M^s(y)$ is, by definition, the probability of the event 'the word printed on output tape after machine M stops coincides with y'; here "s" stands for "stop". A preorder on machines and the notion of a maximal machine are defined as above, and maximal machines do exist. Then $\mathrm{P}_W^s(y)$ calculated for an arbitrary maximal machine W is the a priori probability of y as an element of $\mathbb{B}$. Here it occurs that

$$\left|\log_2 \mathrm{P}_W^s(y)\right| \underset{\cap}{=} \Sigma\mathbb{B}(y).$$

Hence $\Sigma\mathbb{B}$ has a probabilistic semantic too. But, since $\Sigma\mathbb{B} = \mathbf{T}\mathbb{B}$, the entropy $\Sigma\mathbb{B}$ has also an encoding semantic.

1.8 Historical, Bibliographical, and Terminological Remarks; Acknowledgments

We begin the history of the theory of Kolmogorov complexity with Kolmogorov's paper [Kol65]. The purpose of that paper was to bring the notion of complexity (now we should say "of entropy") to the foundations of information theory. In his paper Kolmogorov expounded some results of his studies of 1963–1964. In those years he knew nothing about the paper [Sol64] in which Ray Solomonoff presented some similar ideas — but in vague and rather non-mathematical manner. We place the paper [Sol64] in the prehistory of the theory of Kolmogorov complexity. At the early stage of the theory's development, an important role belonged to the paper [ZL70].

In the papers of pioneers of the theory, there were introduced all five basic entropies of our Sect.1.6. The authors gave them various names and various notations. What was common in all those notations was the use of the letter "K" or the letter "k" as a part of the notation; one should believe the cause of this usage is a homage to Kolmogorov. Here we try to set some system of names and notations with the observance of the historical tradition. (In such a way the author makes his own contribution to the existing chaos of names and notations. This contribution is not too great because some names and notations are already in use. Simultaneously the author expresses the hope to introduce a standard system.)

We would like to fix the following names and notations for the five basic entropies.

1. For $\mathbb{BB}$-entropy. Name: **simple entropy**; notation: KS.
2. For $\mathbb{BT}$-entropy. Name: **decision entropy**; notation: KD.
3. For $\mathbb{TB}$-entropy. Name: **prefix entropy**; notation: KP.
4. For $\mathbb{TT}$-entropy. Name: **monotonic entropy**; notation: KM.
5. For $\Sigma\mathbb{T}$-entropy. Name: **a priori entropy**; notation: KA.

The entropies should be attributed to the following authors:

- simple entropy KS to Kolmogorov [Kol65](§3) and also (though in some nebulous form) to Solomonoff [Sol64],
- decision entropy KD to Loveland [Lov69],
- a priori entropy KA to Levin [ZL70](n° 3.3) and [Lev73],
- monotonic entropy KM to Levin [Lev73], and
- prefix entropy KP to Levin [Lev76].

Remark. Strictly speaking, we denote by the symbols KS, KD, KA, KM and KP exactly those versions of entropies as they were formulated by Kolmogorov, Loveland, and Levin. Let us recall the Important Remark of Sect.1. The coincidence KS with $\mathbb{BB}$ has the following meaning: for any particular entropy KS and for any particular entropy $\mathbb{BB}$, there holds $KS(y) \underset{\cap}{=} \mathbb{BB}(y)$. The other coincidences, KD with $\mathbb{BT}$, etc., are to be understood in the same way.

Attributing the entropies to their inventors, we make no claim about the usage of these notations by the inventors. None of them made any essential use of the term "entropy"; usually the term "complexity" was used. Kolmogorov used simply the word "complexity" with no adjective. Loveland used the term "uniform complexity", and it was renamed as "decision complexity" by Zvonkin and Levin [ZL70](Definition 2.2). Levin used the words "monotonic complexity" and "complexity related to a prefix algorithm". He had not introduced any name for KA, but used terms "universal semicomputable measure" (in [ZL70]($n°$ 3.3)) and "a priori probability" (in [Lev73]) for related quantities of which the logarithm is to be taken.

As to notations, Kolmogorov in [Kol65](§3) employed the notation $K_A(y)$ for the simple entropy. Loveland in [Lov69](p.513) employed the notation $K_A(x^n; n)$ for the decision entropy; and Zvonkin and Levin used for it the notation KR [ZL70](Definition 2.2). Zvonkin and Levin in [ZL70]($n°$ 3.3) employed the notation $-\log_2 R\{\Gamma_x\}$ for the a priori entropy; later, in [Lev73] that entropy was denoted by Levin as kM. In the same paper [Lev73] the notation km was used for the monotonic entropy. The notation KP (for the prefix entropy) appeared in [Lev76].

The general idea of an approximation space as a space of informations refining, or exactifying, one another is, without doubt, due to D. Scott. This idea was embodied into the notion of f_0-space in the sense of Yu. Ershov. A classification of entropies on the basis of that notion is given in [She84](Theorem 8); the classification of our Sect.1.3 is very close to that of [She84]. The general idea of the encoding-free approach to entropies (see Sect.1.5 above) was laid down in [Lev76].

A very useful exposition of various entropies and their interrelation is given in [Vyu81]. A survey of the use of entropies in a definition of randomness is presented in [KU87a] and [KU87b].

In the process of preparing this paper, the author had many discussions with Andrei Muchnik, Alexander Shen', and Nikolai Vereshchagin. The author enjoyed their advice and help. Many final formulations emerged from those thankworthy discussions. The bounds of Sect.2.1 and of Sect.2.2 probably belongs to what is called "mathematical folk-lore", but the final formulae are also due to discussions with Muchnik, Shen', and Vereshchagin.

To conclude this section let us redraw Fig.3 in terms and notations that we accept as standard; Fig.4.

The pentagon of Fig.4 shows, in particular, that neither KA < KS nor KS < KA. The exclamation note attached to an entropy means that the entropy can be used in the Kolmogorov definition of randomness.

2 Quantitative Analysis on Entropies

2.1 Bounds for Entropies

Some upper and lower bounds for entropies will be written down in this section. But first of all the reader must be warned that in this exposition, the sense of an

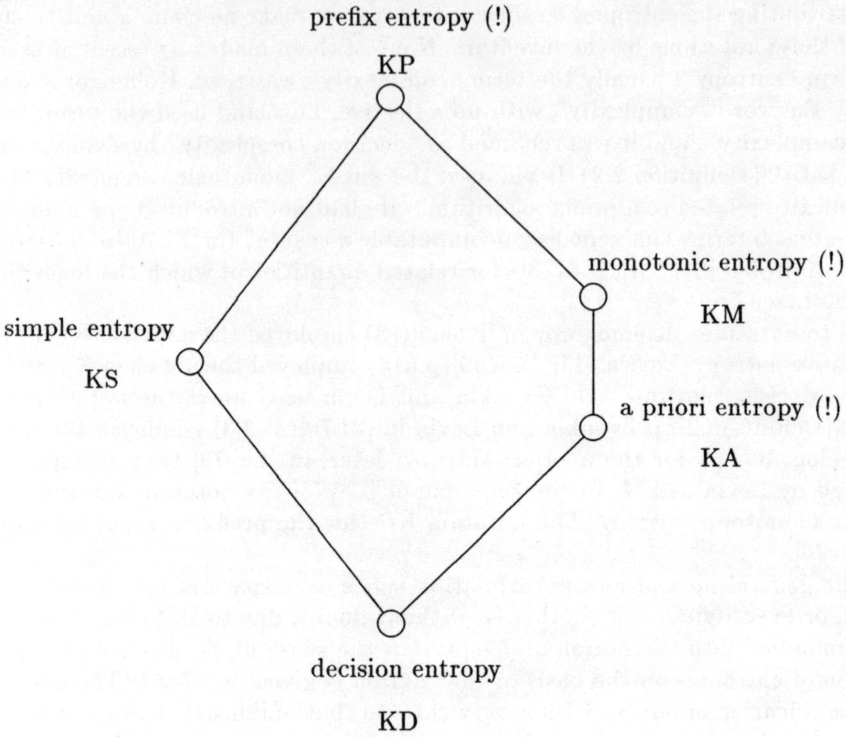

Fig. 4. Five basic entropies

upper bound and the sense of a lower bound are rather different. An upper bound
for an entropy shows that the entropy cannot be too large. A lower bound for an
entropy does not show that the entropy cannot be too small but does show that
in infinitely many instances, the entropy can be large enough. So upper bounds
are absolute, or strong, upper bounds. Lower bounds are not absolute; we shall
call them *weak* lower bounds. A weak lower bound has the purpose of supporting
the corresponding upper bound and demonstrating, in a favorable case, that the
upper bound cannot be improved.

After this warning let us consider the five basic entropies of Sect.1.8, Fig.4.

(1) Entropies KS, KM, KA, and KD.

Let *Ent* denotes one of the entropies KS, KM, KA, KD. Then (an upper
bound) for all y (in Ξ),

$$Ent(y) \underset{\oplus}{\leq} |y|,$$

and (a weak lower bound) for infinitely many y (in Ξ),

$$Ent(y) \underset{\oplus}{\geq} |y|. \tag{1}$$

Let us formulate the lower bound of (1) more exactly. We have four cases: $Ent = KS$, $Ent = KM$, $Ent = KA$, $Ent = KD$. For each of these cases, the symbol Ent (as well as KS, KM, KA or KD) denotes an arbitrary function belonging to some collection, i.e., the collection of Ent-entropies. In each case the meaning of (1) is as follows: for any particular function Ent of that collection, there exist a constant c, perhaps negative, and an infinite set $M \subseteq \Xi$ such that

$$\forall y \in M \, [\, Ent(y) \geq |y| + c \,].$$

(2) **Entropy KP.**

It is helpful to introduce some notation. A function qlog, quasilogarithm, is introduced by the following definition:

$$\mathrm{qlog}\, z = \begin{cases} \log_2 z, & z \geq 1, \\ 0, & z \leq 1. \end{cases}$$

The iterations of that function are defined as follows:

$$\mathrm{qlog}^{(1)} z = \mathrm{qlog}\, z, \quad \text{and} \quad \mathrm{qlog}^{(k+1)} z = \mathrm{qlog}(\mathrm{qlog}^{(k)} z).$$

Then we have for any k, any $\epsilon > 0$, and all y,

$$\mathrm{KP}(y) \underset{\oplus}{\leq} |y| + \mathrm{qlog}^{(1)}|y| + \mathrm{qlog}^{(2)}|y| + \cdots + \mathrm{qlog}^{(k-1)}|y| + (1+\epsilon)\mathrm{qlog}^{(k)}|y|. \tag{2}$$

It is an upper bound for KP.

For a weak lower bound, let k be an arbitrary positive integer. Then, for infinitely many y,

$$[\, \mathrm{KP}(y) \geq |y| + \mathrm{qlog}^{(1)}|y| + \mathrm{qlog}^{(2)}|y| + \cdots + \mathrm{qlog}^{(k)}|y| \,]. \tag{3}$$

That means that inequality (3) holds for any function denoted by KP (i.e. for any prefix entropy) and for an appropriate infinite set of y's, depending on the choice of that function.

Now it is reasonable to introduce an abbreviation for the sum $\mathrm{qlog}^{(1)}z + \cdots + (1+\epsilon)\mathrm{qlog}^{(k)}z$. Let us take, e.g., $Q_k(z,\epsilon)$ as such an abbreviation. That is,

$$Q_k(z,\epsilon) = \mathrm{qlog}^{(1)}z + \mathrm{qlog}^{(2)}z + \cdots + \mathrm{qlog}^{(k-1)}z + (1+\epsilon)\mathrm{qlog}^{(k)}z.$$

Then (2) and (3) can be rewritten as follows:

$$\forall y \, [\, \mathrm{KP}(y) \underset{\oplus}{\leq} |y| + Q_k(|y|,\epsilon) \,],$$

and

$$\text{for infinitely many } y \, [\, \mathrm{KP}(y) \geq |y| + Q_k(|y|,0) \,].$$

2.2 Bounds for Differences of Entropies

By how much can two entropies of different sorts, e.g., KP and KD, can differ from one another? Perhaps it is better to ask, how much can one entropy exceed the other? Upper and lower bounds are to give the answer. The warning of the beginning of Sect.2.1 about the different meanings of upper and lower bounds is valid here and now too.

When $A(y) \stackrel{+}{\leq} B(y)$, an upper bound for the difference $A(y) - B(y)$ is trivial; namely, a constant. So in this section, only differences $A(y) - B(y)$ for which the assertion $A(y) \stackrel{+}{\leq} B(y)$ is false will be studied.

Now let us proceed to the differences.

(1) Difference KP − KD.

   For any k, any $\epsilon > 0$, and all y,

$$KP(y) - KD(y) \stackrel{+}{\leq} q\log|y| + Q_k(|y|, \epsilon). \tag{4}$$

For any k and infinitely many y,

$$KP(y) - KD(y) \geq q\log|y| + Q_k(|y|, 0). \tag{5}$$

Note. Let us not forget that an additive constant implied in (4) depends not only on k and ϵ but also on the particular versions of KP and KD. In (5) the set of y's depends not only on k but also on the versions of KP and KD. This point is valid for further inequalities related to lower and upper bounds.

(2) Differences KS − KM and KS − KA.

   Let $|y| \neq 0$. Then, for all y,

$$KS(y) - KM(y) \stackrel{+}{\leq} KS(y) - KA(y) \stackrel{+}{\leq} \log_2 |y|.$$

For some c and for infinitely many y,

$$KS(y) - KM(y) \geq \log_2 |y| + c \,],$$

and for some c and for infinitely many y,

$$KS(y) - KA(y) \geq \log_2 |y| + c.$$

(3) Differences KM − KS and KA − KS.

   For any k, any $\epsilon > 0$, and all y,

$$KM(y) - KS(y) \stackrel{+}{\leq} Q_k(|y|, \epsilon),$$
$$KA(y) - KS(y) \stackrel{+}{\leq} Q_k(|y|, \epsilon).$$

For any k and infinitely many y,

$$KM(y) - KS(y) \geq Q_k(|y|, 0),$$
$$KA(y) - KS(y) \geq Q_k(|y|, 0).$$

(4) Differences $KP-KS$, $KS-KD$, $KP-KM$, $KP-KA$, $KM-KD$, and $KA-KD$.

Let $B - A$ be any of the six entropy differences mentioned above. For any k, any $\epsilon > 0$, and all y,

$$B(y) - A(y) \underset{\text{fi}}{\leq} Q_k(|y|, \epsilon).$$

And for any k and infinitely many y,

$$B(y) - A(y) \geq Q_k(|y|, 0).$$

(5) The Difference $KM - KA$.

This difference is of special interest. The very fact that the conjecture $KM(y) \underset{\text{fi}}{=} KA(y)$ is false is disappointing. The refutation of that conjecture is due to Petér Gács [Gac83]. (The Hungarian surname "Gács" is to be pronounced as English "garch".)

Both KM and KA are defined on the binary tree $\mathbf{T}$. Gács studied two entropies K and H of similar sorts; but his K and H are defined not on $\mathbf{T}$ but on the tree consisting of all words in a countable alphabet (say, in $\mathbb{N}$ if one takes $\mathbb{N}$ as an alphabet). Some bound for the difference $K - H$ is stated in Theorem 1.1 of [Gac83]; there the author writes: "Therefore for binary strings, the lower bound obtainable from the proof of Theorem 1.1 is only the inverse of some version of Ackermann's function" [Gac83](p.75). As it is known, Ackermann's function is a function from $\mathbb{N}$ to $\mathbb{N}$ which exceeds in its growth any primitive recursive function. The inverse f^{-1} for a function f is defined as follows:

$$f^{-1}(a) = \min\{z : f(z) \geq a\}.$$

Thus, for infinitely many y,

$$KM(y) - KA(y) \geq f^{-1}(|y|), \tag{6}$$

where f is the version of Ackermann's function mentioned by Gács.

Let $Z(y)$ denote the number of zeros in the word y. Then, as a corollary of Theorem 1.1 of [Gac83], we have the following: for any k and for any m, there exists a $y \in \Xi$ such that $Z(y) > m$ and

$$KM(y) - KA(y) \geq Q_k(Z(y), 0). \tag{7}$$

Therefore, we have two weak lower bounds. As to upper bounds, there is known no one except the following trivial one: for any k, any $\epsilon > 0$, and all y,

$$KM(y) - KA(y) \underset{\text{fi}}{\leq} Q_k(|y|, \epsilon). \tag{8}$$

Since the weak lower bounds (6) and (7) do not support the upper bound (8), the task of improving all those bounds is open.

References

[Gac83]   P. Gács. On the relation between descriptional complexity and algorithmic probability. *Theoretical Computer Science* 22:71–93, 1983.

[Kol65]   A. N. Kolmogorov. Three approaches to the quantitative definition of information. *Problems Inform. Transmission* 1:1–7, 1965. (Translated from the Russian version.)

[Kol68]   A. N. Kolmogorov. Logical basis for information theory and probability theory. *IEEE Trans. on Information Theory* IT-14.5:662–664, 1969. (The Russian version exists.)

[KU87a]   A. N. Kolmogorov and V. A. Uspensky. Algorithms and randomness. In *Proc. 1st World Congress of the Bernoulli Society*, vol. 1, Yu. A. Prohorov and V. V. Sazonov, (eds.), VNU Science Press, Utrecht 3–53, 1987.

[KU87b]   A. N. Kolmogorov and V. A. Uspensky. Algorithms and randomness. *Theory Probab. Appl.* 32:389–412, 1987. (Translated from the Russian version.) (*Comment:* There are two regrettable errors in the English version: p.394, line 2 from the bottom, and p.395, lines 1 and 3 from the top, the word "countable" must be replaced by "enumerable (i.e. recursively enumerable)"; p.395, line 1 from the top, the word "in" must be removed.)

[Lev73]   L. A. Levin. On the notion of a random sequence. *Soviet Math. Dokl.* 14:1413–1416, 1973. (Translated from the Russian version.)

[Lev76]   L. A. Levin. Various measures of complexity for finite objects (axiomatic description). *Soviet Math. Dokl.* 17:522–526, 1976. (Translated from the Russian version.)

[Lov69]   D. W. Loveland. A variant of the Kolmogorov concept of complexity. *Information and Control* 15:510–526, 1969.

[Mar66]   P. Martin-Lof. On the definition of random sequences. *Information and Control* 9:602–619, 1966.

[She84]   A. Kh. Shen'. Algorithmic variants of the notion of entropy. *Soviet Math. Dokl.* 29:569–573, 1984. (Translated from the Russian version.) (*Comment:* There are many misprints in the English version.)

[Sol64]   R. Solomonoff. A formal theory of inductive inference, Part I. *Information and Control* 7:1–22, 1964.

[US81]   V. A. Uspensky and A. L. Semenov. What are the gains of the theory of algorithms: basic developments connected with the concept of algorithm and with its applications in mathematics (Part I,§17). In Springer-Verlag, Lecture Notes in Computer Science 122:100-234, 1981.

[US87]   V. A. Uspensky and A. L. Semenov. *Teoria algoritmov: osnovnye otkrytiya i prilozheniya* (Theory of algorithms: main discoveries and applications) (§1.17). Nauka, Moscow, 1987; in Russian.

[Vyu81]   V. V. V'yugin. Algorithmic entropy (complexity) of finite objects and its application to defining randomness and quantity of information. *Semiotika i Informatika* (Semiotics and Informatics) 16:14–43, 1981; in Russian.

[ZL70]   A. K. Zvonkin and L. A. Levin. The complexity of finite objects and the development of the concepts of information and randomness by means of the theory of algorithms. *Russian Math. Surveys* 25:83–124, 1970. (Translated from the Russian version.)

Subject Index

Printing: Mercedesdruck, Berlin
Binding: Buchbinderei Lüderitz & Bauer, Berlin

EATCS Monographs on Theoretical Computer Science

R. Janicki, P. E. Lauer
**Specification and Analysis of
Concurrent Systems**
The COSY Approach

O. Watanabe (Ed.)
**Kolmogorov Complexity
and Computational Complexity**

K. Jensen
Coloured Petri Nets
Basic Concepts, Analysis Methods
and Practical Use, Vol. 1